JUDAH NATION

a people of praise

CLINT BROWN

LEGACY
PUBLISHERS INTERNATIONAL

• • •

Unless otherwise indicated, all Scripture quotations are from the Authorized King James Version of the Bible

Judah Nation: A People of Praise
ISBN 1-880809-67-2

Legacy Publishers International
1301 South Clinton Street
Denver, CO 80247
www.legacypublishersinternational.com

2 3 4 5 6 7 8 9 19 11 12 13 / 13 12 11 10 09 08 07

• • •

Dedication

"JUDAH NATION" is dedicated to every musician, singer, and song writer that I've had the privilege to work with over the past 20 years. From my start in Richie, Louisiana as a teenager...through today...all of you have been a blessing in my life.

We're all a part of the same nation...Judah Nation.

Thank you,

Pastor Clint Brown

• • •

• • •

Table of Contents

	Introduction vii
Chapter 1	God With A Need 1
Chapter 2	The Path to Praise .11
Chapter 3	The Product of Praise 21
Chapter 4	I Got It in the Middle 29
Chapter 5	Sound Advice 39
Chapter 6	Behind the Music 47
Chapter 7	Mouth Alert! 59
Chapter 8	Canceled by Complaint 71
Chapter 9	This Praise Is for You 83
Chapter 10	The Price of Praise 93
Chapter 11	Can I Catch A Ride? 101
Chapter 12	Keys to the Gate .109
Chapter 13	Building A Habitation of Praise 117
Chapter 14	It's All Downhill From Here! 127
Chapter 15	Just Give Him the Praise 137
Chapter 16	How's Your Night Life? 145
Chapter 17	A Simple Thank You Will Do 153
	About the Author .161

• • •

...

Introduction

Have you ever been driving home but suddenly had to take a detour? And then the unthinkable…a flat tire! You're stuck in transition, headed for your destination, but caught in a place where you don't want to be. The problem for many people is that when they get into that situation in their life, they think that's where they're supposed to be. So they stay there complaining about where they've ended up. "I can't believe I ended up here; I can't believe I have to deal with this." And they lay down their praise based upon their problem and they're sitting in their situation wondering where God is.

We are a generation of thankless people. There are people who are constantly focused on what they have or what they do not have, but wish they did. We are a people who remember our pain more than we do our victories. We remember our struggles more than we remember our successes. It's easy for us to live in a state of depression because we live in a nation that is depressed with the information of pain and wars and struggle and trouble and trial.

• • •

We mark our level of happiness and fulfillment and thankful-ness based on what somebody else has and what we don't have. You can have a million dollars in the bank and still be bankrupt of peace. You can live in a 10,000 square foot house, but live in an empty home.

You have to learn to go back and pick up your praise wherever you left it and bring it to the situation where you are now and start giving Him the praise. When you start praising Him, that's when deliverance shows up. That's when abundance and blessing show up. Every day you live you are going to face situations, but if you don't let them steal your praise, then your praise will catapult you through every problem you encounter.

Your praise has possessing power. Your praise has releasing power. Ask Paul and Silas in Acts 16 when they were chained to the prison walls. Paul said, "I've got a key; it's called praise!" And praise unlocked the jail. Praise will turn your life completely around. As long as you've got a praise, you've got a future. As long as you've got a praise, you've got a promise from God.

You can turn your situation into a place of praise. And wherev-er your praise is, God shows up in your circumstances. Most of us let distance get between God and us and the only time He hears our voice is when we are in trouble. But God inhabits the sound of your heart and gratitude. The farther you get from your problem and the closer you get to God, your mentality will change from "It SHALL BE well," to "It IS well." When you build a place of praise, there will come a time when all you see is God.

Praise is not an intention of the heart or a meditation of the mind. Praise is, *"Let every thing that hath breath praise the Lord,"* (Psalm 150:6) or Let anybody breathing make the sound of grati-tude to be heard.

• • •

You must understand that your praise is going to cost you something. Your praise is going to make you do things you never dreamed you'd ever do. Your praise will send you into situations you never thought you'd walk into. Your praise will make you do something that everybody said you could never accomplish. Your praise will look toward the battle and into the face of the devil whenever circumstances are coming against you.

There are many things I think about when I think about God. Of all the things I think about Him, lack is certainly not one of them! I always think about His provision. I always think about what He has. I mean, I would never think about God in terms of insufficient funds or of Him not being able to do something. We're talking about the Man who spoke the worlds into existence! He didn't buy them; He spoke them! When you can speak worlds into existence, you aren't wanting for much! And yet, He is searching for something. In John 4:23 His Word tells us, *"But the hour cometh, and now is, when the true worshippers shall worship the Father in spirit and in truth: for the Father seeketh such to worship him."* God is searching for those who will worship Him.

Every once in a while I'll receive a card from somebody and it will say, "What do you give a man who has everything?" Sometimes I look at God and go through my day asking Him to do things for me. Help me, God, do this. God make a way. God open this door. God bring finances for this. And I do that because I know He is a God with nothing lacking. But I did discover that God has a need that only I can fill. He didn't put it in the animals or birds. He did not put it in the trees. He put it into us. The only thing God has need of is for somebody to fill the void that was made when Lucifer left Him as the worship leader of all the kingdoms of light resounding through the heavens, lifting up His name. And now you have that honor.

• • •

Don't let a day go by that you don't give God, not only what He deserves, but what He needs.

My issue should never be a match for my praise! *"...Eye hath not seen, nor ear heard, neither have entered into the heart of man, the things which God hath prepared for them that love him."* (1 Corinthians 2:9) That tells me that I haven't even begun to imagine all that God has in store for me! I don't know about you, but the best is yet to come in my life! And I believe the very best is yet to come in yours as well!

• • •

Chapter 1

God With A Need

W hen I was recording my first album in Orlando, *Night of Destiny,* I was gone for hours upon hours at a time. I was doing everything. I did all the music and the background vocals and I was producing it and writing it, too. I'd get home at two or three o'clock in the morning. My kids would be asleep. Then the next morning I'd wake up, but by then they were already gone to school and doing their stuff, going through their day. After about four nights straight of not seeing them, I walked into my house to just cuddle down in my favorite chair and relax for a few minutes. I thought everybody was asleep in their beds, but I was wrong. My little girl, Tori, had stayed in my favorite chair. I walked over to her and there she was. She had a blanket over her. She knew where I liked to sit when I came home, so she had positioned herself where she knew her father would be.

So I walked in and when I looked at her in the chair, I saw something in her hand, and I pulled it out. It was a little piece of paper

• • •

and it said, "To Daddy." When I opened it, I don't think there were three words spelled right. But you know when your kids leave you a note, it doesn't matter what it says, or how it's spelled!

* * *

"Dear Daddy,

I know that you're working real hard every night, but I miss you.

And if you would wake me up and kiss me goodnight, I would love that.

Love, Tori

I'm waiting on you."

* * *

At that moment, I found out that bicycles and Barbie dolls and clothes and things like that, that was all stuff she *wanted*, but I was what she *needed*.

For the Son of man is come to save that which was lost. (Matthew 18:11)

I think about God a lot, about His greatness, His amazing love, His abundance of grace and loving kindness. There are many things I think about God, but lack is never one of them! When I think about Him, it just never crosses my mind to think in terms of lack or insufficient funds or of His not being able to do something! We're talking about the One who spoke the worlds into existence. When you can do that, you're not lacking for anything!

So I find a God who is not in lack. He's not a God who's lacking what we need in our everyday lives. He has everything. But, the Bible does talk about Him searching and looking for something that was lost. Now, in Haggai 2:8 we read where God says, "The silver is mine. The gold is mine." He said everything there is that brings riches is His. Then again in Psalm 50:10-12 He says, *"For every beast of the forest is mine, and the cattle upon a thousand hills. I know all the fowls of the mountains: and the wild beasts of the field are mine. If I were hungry, I would not tell thee: for the world is mine, and the fulness thereof."*

Now, don't get me wrong. You must know that God is not in a state of emergency. God's not in a recession. He's not watching the DOW, following His stocks. He's not on the computer every night checking all of His investments. Wall Street is not affecting Him. He's not moved by any of that because He's not a God of lack. That's not what He's after, but the Scriptures tell us that He is searching for something.

God's not missing gold and silver. He's not missing cattle or beasts or fowls of the air. He said those things are plenteous, but there's still something more. Something's gone. So I began to look and I thought, *Well, maybe it's man.* But it's not man because man was redeemed through the blood of Christ.

Going back further into the Bible, I found Ezekiel 28:13-16.

Thou hast been in Eden the garden of God; every precious stone was thy covering, the sardius, topaz, and the diamond, the beryl, the onyx, and the jasper, the sapphire, the emerald, and the carbuncle, and gold: the workmanship of thy tabrets and of thy pipes was prepared in thee in the day that thou wast created. Thou art the anointed cherub that covereth; and I have set thee so: thou wast upon the holy mountain of God; thou hast walked up and down in the midst of the stones of fire. Thou wast perfect in thy ways from the day thou wast created, till iniquity was found in thee. By the multitude of thy merchandise they have filled the midst of thee with violence, and thou hast sinned: therefore I will

• • •

cast thee as profane out of the mountain of God: and I will destroy thee, O covering cherub, from the midst of the stones of fire.

In other words, God said everything was beautiful and prepared. It was first class; it was done right. Jesus' rendition of what Ezekiel saw went like this, *"I beheld Satan as lightning fall from heaven."* (Luke 10:18) He didn't roll out of heaven or skip or jog or float out of heaven. That guy fell as fast as light!

You must understand that before he was expelled from the heavenlies, Satan (Lucifer) was designed and crafted for something that God had in the heavenlies. He was ordained and positioned in the mountain of God. The mountain of God is the place of Zion that brings forth praise and brings forth worship. Everything in Satan was designed especially for the atmosphere of worship. He had rhythmic tools built into his being surrounded by jewels and precious stones. When he walked, he had to have been the original jam-box all in one! Every time he moved, every time he breathed, music came out of him, giving God the praise.

And so he walked through heaven and as he did, every move he made brought rhythm. Every time he breathed and exhaled, it led the choirs of heaven into a resounding sound saying, "Holy! Holy! Holy!" When he turned to his left, it would change keys and modulate and somebody would say, "Worthy, worthy, worthy!" And when he turned to the right, somebody would say, "Righteous! Righteous! Righteous!" And when he turned again, they'd say, "King of kings and Lord of lords!" And then he'd turn and voices would cry, "Prince of peace! Mighty God!" What a powerful praise. What a powerful worship. It was filling the heavenlies and permeating the atmosphere.

But something happened and the Bible says that God was sitting there and Jesus said, "I didn't have anything to do with it. I was just chilling there and I saw Lucifer—there one minute and gone the

• • •

next, just dismissed from heaven." And for the first time since eternity and the beginning existed—silence. No music. No worship. And God sat there on His throne, and said, "Something is needed. I need something. I must have it."

Then God bent down to the dust of the earth, and He created a man. He made man just like Himself. Then God breathed life into man, and as he breathed, Adam's eyes popped open. And God and Adam stood together. And the Bible says they worshipped in the cool of the day.

You have to see that worship is more than just singing a song. Worship is relationship and intimacy together. And so they would sit there in the cool of the day. And as they were together there, God said to his man, "Hey, all of this is yours. I don't need anything. I've got everything I need. I just need to hear your praise and worship like this." All He needed to hear was somebody restoring what had just been lost.

> Worship is relationship and intimacy together.

Something happened in the garden of perfection. All of a sudden, slithering down the trees, through the bushes and through the grass, Satan found God's replacement just like he does all the time. Most of the greatest talent that stands on stages right now singing for the devil are talent that used to sing on a platform in somebody's church. Satan's influence took man and separated him from God.

First John 3:8 says, *"For this purpose the Son of God was manifested, that he might destroy the works of the devil."* And then one day Jesus found himself sitting on a well. We find the story in John 4:6-29. (This is my paraphrased version of what took place.) He's just sitting there and a woman carrying a bucket walks up to Him. He looks at her and says, "What's up? How you doin'?"

• • •

She said, "I'd like some water if you could get off that well. I'll get me some water."

He said, "You don't realize you're talking to a well sitting on a well. You came here for natural nourishment, but let Me just tell you something. Let me qualify Myself in your life and let you know that I know some stuff. You've already been through five men, and the guy you're with right now is not your husband. You're not married; you're shacked up."

You know what I love so much about Jesus? He didn't condemn her. Instead, He just said, "Hey, don't do that any longer. And by the way, if you would ask Me for a drink today, I would give you a drink and you would never thirst again!"

And she went crazy. She said, "Oh! I've got to tell somebody!" And she started off back to the city.

But Jesus reached out, grabbed her, and stopped her and asked, "Where are you going?"

"They're all worshipping at the temple. I've got to go tell them!" she answered.

"No, no, no," He said. "They don't even know what they're doing."

That's like a lot of churches today. "They don't know what they're even worshipping over. They don't have a clue. But the hour is coming…in fact, it's here…where the true worshippers are going to worship Him in spirit and in truth. The Father is seeking somebody!"

On another day, Jesus came walking through the city. It's recorded in Luke 10:38-42.

Now it came to pass, as they went, that he entered into a certain village: and a certain woman named Martha received him

• • •

into her house. And she had a sister called Mary, which also sat at Jesus' feet, and heard his word. But Martha was cumbered about much serving, and came to him, and said, Lord, dost thou not care that my sister hath left me to serve alone? bid her therefore that she help me. And Jesus answered and said unto her, Martha, Martha, thou art careful and troubled about many things: But one thing is needful: and Mary hath chosen that good part, which shall not be taken away from her.

There was Martha, cooking and working and getting all her stuff together. You know she's wondering, "Let's see…He's been eating a lot of carbs lately. Some Diet Pepsi or Diet Coke. That's what He needs. He needs something to drink to refresh Him, something to eat…" She's serving. And serving. And serving! And you know how it is when a woman starts working and other folks aren't doing anything! They didn't talk in "thee's" and "thou's." Mary's just sitting there at the feet of Jesus, and Martha says, "Jesus, I've been serving and serving and working. And I've been working in the church and I've been working for the Lord and working for the Lord and working for the Lord."

Yes, but do you know the Lord of the work? Jesus just said, "Yeah, but Martha, you need this part that Mary's chosen, sitting before Me. This shall not ever be taken away from her." This is what the Father's seeking.

In Luke 7:37-50 we have yet another story of Jesus and a woman. Jesus was in the house of Simon the leper, having a meal. He comes into the room and sits down. The disciples are there as well. When all of a sudden from the back of the room comes a woman with her head down because she has lived in shame for selling herself to put food on the table for her babies. She knows she doesn't deserve anything, but she takes the most valuable thing she

• • •

has, an alabaster box of expensive ointment, and falls at His feet. I like Luke's account of what she did: *"And* (she) *stood at his feet behind him weeping, and began to wash his feet with tears, and did wipe them with the hairs of her head, and kissed his feet, and anointed them with the ointment."* What a beautiful picture of worship. Her actions said that she didn't have much and didn't feel worthy, but she was bringing to Him and giving to Him the best that she had. And she bowed herself down before Him. Those disciples present were upset that she would "waste" such a valuable commodity that could have been sold to care for the poor. But Jesus was touched…what the Father seeketh for…by this woman's heart gesture. And He said that her story would forever be for a memorial. And He told her, "Your sins are forgiven."

> What would happen if all of His children woke up tomorrow morning and just said, "I give you praise, Lord. I praise Your name.

God inhabits the praises of His people. He desires to hear His children lift up their voices and give Him praise. Your alarm clock just rang. It's 6:00 in the morning, and He sits on the edge of His throne, and He waits. And when you raise your head off the pillow of rest, you get up, and you shake your head, and you brush your teeth, and you take your shower, and you do your hair and your makeup, and you put your clothes on. You've got it all together and He goes, "See you later. Have a good day. I hope all is well." He moves over to the next house. He waits anxiously. They wake up and go through the same routines. "See you later."

What would happen if all of His children woke up tomorrow morning and just said, "I give you praise, Lord. I praise Your name. While I'm tying my shoes I want to thank You for the ability just to

• • •

get up out of my bed. Kids, you all have a good day and remember while you're at school, Mama's going to be right here giving God praise. I'll see you, baby. Have a good flight. I'll just be right here lifting up the praise." All He needs is your praise. All He needs is your worship. What heaven lost, He has found in you. Every time you lift your hands and open up your mouth, he says, "I found what I've been looking for!"

The thing I love about praise and worship is, if God inhabits praise, then when He shows up everything that's fighting against you is going to be dealt with by Him. That means that somebody may ask you one day, "How did you ever get delivered from that?" And you can say, "You know, it was one Thursday afternoon. I just started singing. It started with a song, but then the song went to my soul. I was walking around the house just saying, 'You're worthy of praise,' and something hit me at the top of my head and went to the soles of my feet and changed my body. And I knew that cancer died in the midst of my praise!" When God shows up, we can say with David, *"Let God arise, and his enemies be scattered."* (Psalm 68:1)

• • •

...

Chapter 2

The Path to Praise

This people have I formed for myself; they shall shew forth my praise. (Isaiah 43:21) There is a path to praise.

Have you ever been trying to go somewhere and you get directions that sound something like this? "Take highway 47, then you're goin' to go down there a ways and you'll see a Wal-Mart. Don't turn there! Just keep on goin'! Now, you're goin' to come to highway 27; take a right. Then you're goin' to run over some railroad tracks and then there'll be a red barn on the left, but don't worry about that...." You know the directions I'm talking about! Sometimes the hardest thing for us to do is to follow directions. You've been given directions like these before by people who give you everything in between that doesn't matter. In fact, all those details can be downright distracting. Truth is, it doesn't really matter whether you notice that red barn or not because it's not part of the end result.

• • •

God doesn't give us all the details of our journey. If He did, many of us would never leave where we are. He put Joseph to sleep and showed him a dream in which Joseph was in a palace with others bowing down to him, a place of power. But God never showed Joseph the pit! When Joseph was down in that pit, can't you just hear him saying, "I'm out of God's will because this part right here wasn't in that dream!" Then he leaves the pit and ends up at Potiphar's house and then gets slammed into prison, but he didn't see it coming because he didn't see the prison. God just doesn't give us all the details! He knows that would overwhelm us. But He knows where our destiny is to be. So He creates things in our lives that form us and move us toward our destiny. He doesn't give us all the facts, but He lets us know that there are issues within those journeys that are going to cause us to want to quit.

Jesus said it this way, in John 16:33:

These things I have spoken unto you, that in me ye might have peace. In the world ye shall have tribulation: but be of good cheer; I have overcome the world.

Paul talked about it in Romans 5:1-5:

Therefore being justified by faith, we have peace with God through our Lord Jesus Christ: By whom also we have access by faith into this grace wherein we stand, and rejoice in hope of the glory of God. And not only so, but we glory in tribulations also: knowing that tribulation worketh patience; And patience, experience; and experience, hope: And hope maketh not ashamed; because the love of God is shed abroad in our hearts by the Holy Ghost which is given unto us.

We get all excited about the part where we get to stand and rejoice in hope of the glory of God. That sounds great! But then he

• • •

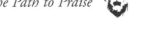

flips it on us when he says, "not only so, but glory in tribulation." He tells us about peace and about hope and all these things, but then he says, "Oh, and by the way, glory in tribulation, knowing that tribulation works patience."

God never gives us the middle of the road, just the beginning and the end of the road. In Romans 8:27 Paul makes this statement:

> *And he that searcheth the hearts knoweth what is the mind of the Spirit, because he maketh intercession for the saints according to the will of God.*

Do you realize today that God has a plan for your life? As you go along in your life, you're going to find those places where you thought you knew what was best in a situation. But then, as you continue to move toward that decision, you realize that it is not really God's will and it's not really working out. And you have to let God redirect you. We don't flow in God's will for our lives by sitting there waiting for

> **We don't flow in God's will for our lives by sitting there waiting for something to happen...**

something to happen, waiting for Him to do something. There are too many people sitting around today waiting for God to do it and then reveal it to them. No, God wants to see you doing something.

Some of you men are praying for a wife, but you don't even have a job! You couldn't get a credit card today if you needed one. If you can't do something as simple as that, why do you think any woman should attach her life to yours? You're waiting around for the Lord to send it to you...no, no, no! God gave Adam a job before He gave him a wife! You have to get up and start doing something with what you've got and then let God provide in your life what you don't

• • •

have. It's a journey and so Paul said, "According to His will, he prays that we be conformed to the will of God so we can ultimately bear the image of God."

When Jesus was on the earth, he was not the most celebrated individual there was. Everything wasn't rosy for him. Not everyone praised or worshipped him. His birth wasn't celebrated every December 25. No, he walked through times of rejection. He walked through times of betrayal. He walked through times of denial. He walked through times when people looked at him as an outcast. He had to go out into wilderness issues to be able to get his structure and his anointing in the right place.

You are no different. You may have gone to church, got saved, and feel like you got the Holy Ghost. You may be walking around, speaking like you're a child of the King…and it's good to do all that…but you're not going to bypass and you're not going to miss out on the trials, tribulations, and difficulties of life. Life happens whether you're saved or unsaved. It rains on the just and on the unjust. (Matt. 5:45)

The Bible says two men built a house, one on a rock, one on the sand. Then God sent the flood and the house built on the rock withstood the storm while the one on sand fell to utter destruction. (Luke 6:48) God brings us through times of trouble in our lives so we can demonstrate what He can trust us with. It is not so that we can walk out of it and just be able to say we survived. The intention is that when we come out of it we look a little more like Him than we did before we went into it.

In 1 Peter 5:6 we read, *"Humble yourselves therefore under the mighty hand of God, that he may exalt you in due time."* Also 2 Chronicles 7:14 says, *"If my people, which are called by my name, shall humble themselves, and pray, and seek my face, and turn from their wicked ways; then will I hear from heaven, and will forgive their sin,*

• • •

and will heal their land." Do you realize that God has a way of cutting you down to size? You may think you look good now and have folks fooled around you, but you know who you really are. Humbling yourself will keep you honest and real.

To gain a deeper understanding of this path to praise, let's go back into Isaiah chapter 43. In verse 15 He says, *"I am the Lord, your Holy One, the creator of Israel."* We are always trying to label people's actions as to who they are. Your very first thing to spot in somebody is *Who are you?* Are they who they say they are or are they playing a role for you so that you don't really know the true person you're dealing with? God said here, "I'm not a duplicator and I'm not an imitator. I'm a *creator.* I put you together; I formed you."

In verses 16-18, God tells them:

Thus saith the Lord, which maketh a way in the sea, and a path in the mighty waters; Which bringeth forth the chariot and horse, the army and the power; they shall lie down together, they shall not rise: they are extinct, they are quenched as tow. Remember ye not the former things, neither consider the things of old.

This is what I love about God. Before He leads me into my next fight, He reminds me of how the last one ended! Notice what He said: The chariot and the horse and the might men, they were covered by the sea and they are extinct. He's saying, "That means that I eliminated what you were fighting with earlier! Before you walk into the next fight, I just want to tap you on the shoulder and tell you that if I did it then, I can still do it right now!" You might have to walk through it, but God's going to do it!

Don't you find it interesting that in the same sentence where God is telling them not to remember the former things, He's also reminding them of those very things? Or so it seems because He

• • •

talks about the chariots and horses and the powerful men who came against them. But notice that He's reminding them of what He did. He doesn't want you to start thinking about what you did. You were scared. Yeah, you got all nervous and started whining and complaining and murmuring. It was you who started saying, "I wish we were back in Egypt." It was you who started rehearsing all the good things you had back in bondage. But God said not to remember the former things—don't re-do what you did, but let Me re-do what I did. Oh, we're on the path to praise now!

In verse 19 He says, *"Behold..."* That word means *look at this, check this out.* He said, *"...I will do a new thing; now it shall spring forth; shall ye not know it? I will even make a way in the wilderness, and rivers in the desert. The beast of the field shall honour me, the dragons and the owls: because I give waters in the wilderness, and rivers in the desert, to give drink to my people, my chosen. This people have I formed for myself; they shall shew forth my praise."* He's a God who builds anticipation and expectation. He says, "Hey y'all, you've never seen anything like this before." How many of you are tired of your old stuff, your old house, your old property, your old job. You're ready for a new level.

> ...there is significance in the way God talks to you.

Well, there is significance in the way God talks to you. Here God is talking "farmer talk." He says He will do a new thing and it's going to spring forth. In the Hebrew this is speaking from the farmer's perspective which says it shall spring forth just as a seed that was planted gives way to its harvest. God says you're going to get there, but before you get there, it was already started.

Some of you don't see God doing anything in your life because you haven't experienced it springing forth yet. But just because you

• • •

can't see it doesn't mean it isn't there. I can take you to Louisiana to soybean fields and I can drive you by those fields the day after they're planted. And I can ask you if you see it and you say, "No, I can't see anything but an empty field." But just because you don't see those seeds in there doesn't mean they are not there! Some of you need to realize that you keep stepping on your seed and mashing it down. Some of you keep over-watering it. You keep walking right past it, but God says to position yourself for it because it's already under there and He wants you to recognize it when it happens.

Notice He asks a question, "Shall ye not know it?" The original translation is more like "Shall you not see it and make a note of it?" He's telling you that He's doing a new thing, something you've never seen before. He's about to provide it, about to let you know it. He put it up under your future so you could walk into it and He wants you to note it, write it down. Why would he want you to do that? Because there are things you will go through when He doesn't give you the details. Because He doesn't give you the middle. He just gives you the beginning and the end. And so He wants you to have it written down so when you get to the middle of it and you can't see it because of the situation and the trouble, you still have it written down that all things work together for good to them that love the Lord. All the hits, all the stuff in the middle, are there to help conform you to His image so that when you come to your destination, you look like He looks. You've got a path to take!

Also in verse 19 He tells you two things you're going to experience. He said he'd make a way in the wilderness. That word *wilderness* in the Hebrew means *isolation, solitaire, to shake.* "I will make a way in the shaking. I will provide an escape or a path during the shaking." Then He said He would provide rivers in the desert. The word *desert* means *desolation or a dry place.* As I was reading in the

• • •

original text of this verse I found the word *desert* to also mean *courtroom, dungeon, winter house, palace, prison, temple.* It means *within and without.* So, God said, "I will make a path during the shaking whether you're in the palace or whether you're in the prison, whether you're within or without, whether you're in a dungeon or even a courtroom. No matter where you find yourself, I'm going to make a river for you." A river has an inlet and an outlet. He's saying, "I'm going to cause your dry time to have a beginning, but you hold on because it's going to scoot its way out as well!"

But there's more! That word also means *door.* He said, "I'm going to take you into these issues, but not just to keep you there. I'm taking you there so that when you get there you understand this is just the next level to another door to be opened. But before you walk through this door, remember what I did at the last fight and you won't be afraid to step into your new season. Remember how I treated your enemy in your last season.

Look at verse two in this same chapter of Isaiah.

When thou passest through the waters, I will be with thee; and through the rivers, they shall not overflow thee: when thou walkest through the fire, thou shalt not be burned; neither shall the flame kindle upon thee.

Notice that it says *when* you pass through. It's not optional. It's going to happen. God is saying that not only is it going to happen to you, but you are going to get through it! He says that when you pass through this situation, you're going to face some rivers, but you're going to get through it. You're going to come up to some fires, but you'll get through each one.

Let your attitude on this path to praise be, "I'm going to make it through life's obstacles and situations. I'm not getting bitter; I'm

• • •

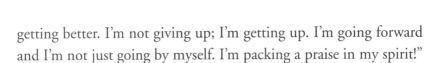

getting better. I'm not giving up; I'm getting up. I'm going forward and I'm not just going by myself. I'm packing a praise in my spirit!"

Verse 21 says, *"This people have I formed for myself; they shall shew forth my praise."* Do you know what a form does? In construction, when you push cement against the form, the form goes "Stop!" It keeps the cement from going where you don't want it to go. The form is what keeps you in place so a foundation can be established. You can't build anything without a foundation under you. And He said that this people have I formed for Myself that they shall show forth MY praise.

What is the path to praise? Shaking and slapping, burning, walking over, through, pushing, getting through and stepped on, stepped over, pushed aside, counted out, talked about, stabbed in the back. The path is people who turn on you, people who don't want to help you, people who act like they don't owe you anything, people you've forgiven who act like it never happened. You want to remind them, but you've already forgiven them! You're just getting through the form. You're just going through it so that at the end of it you can give Him a praise.

If I take a Coke can and shake it up mightily. I shake it up and drop it and kick it and keep shaking it. And then I pull the tab to open it! What was in the can? Coke. And what came out of the can? Coke. And why did Coke come out? It didn't come out because I was shaking the can. No! Coke came out because that's what was put in it before the shaking took place! What comes out of you during your shaking is going to be determined by what's been put into you before the shaking ever begins. And God says He's looking for some people who, after the shaking happens, will have praise come up out of their lips because praise was what was put into them before the shaking started. He's looking for those who will say, "I don't know

• • •

why I went through it, but I'm glad I did because where would I be without it!" Don't worry about the shaking when it starts. It's going to be alright! Just keep praising Him! You're on the path of praise!

• • •

Chapter 3

The Product of Praise

It was February of 1992. I was in a head-on collision in Columbus, Ohio. The impact was horrific and the young lady who hit me died instantly. For a period of time I was paralyzed from the waist down. Walking through that experience I learned that the devil had really wanted both of us to die in the crash. And I learned how to praise God, not just for the things I can see, but also for the things that I cannot. I praise God because I probably should be dead…but I'm not dead!

> *Praise ye the LORD. Praise God in his sanctuary: praise him in the firmament of his power. Praise him for his mighty acts: praise him according to his excellent greatness. Praise him with the sound of the trumpet: praise him with the psaltery and harp. Praise him with the timbrel and dance: praise him with stringed instruments and organs. Praise him upon the loud cymbals: praise him upon the high sounding cymbals. Let every thing that hath breath praise the LORD. Praise ye the LORD.* (Psalm 150)

• • •

In this particular passage, God is not giving us a suggestion. God is giving us a commandment. I believe that as David was penning this psalm, he started out with just a personal thing. He started with "Praise the Lord" because that was personal for him. It was normal. Then he said, "Praise God in the sanctuary" because that was the place where they were to congregate to praise Him. (We know that today, the sanctuary is not the place that David built or the place where any group meets, but the real sanctuary is us.) "Praise Him in the firmament (that's the spirit of His power.). John 4:23 tells us that God is looking for those who will worship Him in spirit and in truth. Next David says, "Praise Him for His mighty acts."

I can see David sitting there saying, "Hey, I'm going to praise God for stuff that I can see that He's doing. He woke me up this morning. He started me on my way. I've got eyes to see. I've got ears to hear." Praise Him for the things you can see. Those are the mighty acts. Those are the delivering hands of God. And then David goes on to say, "Praise Him according to his excellent greatness." That's the stuff you don't see. That's the stuff you can't see, just like my accident. That's the place where you realize, "Whoa, I should have been dead ten years ago." That's where you come to recognize that the truck should have hit your child and it didn't, or that the wreck should have killed you, but you're still alive.

In verses 3-5 David calls us to praise with all manner of musical instrument and dance. David was drawing from his personal experiences, so he must have been used to raising quite a ruckus in his praising at times! Think about it. If you can be loud at a ball game, if you can be loud at the Hard Rock Café or the House of Blues, then it ought to be okay to get loud in the House of God!

David finishes the psalm off by saying that, bottom line, if you're breathing, then get to praising Him! We don't praise Him to

• • •

hear ourselves. But every time something comes out of our mouth, it produces something. It has a life on its own. Proverbs 18:20-21 puts it like this. *"A man's belly shall be satisfied with the fruit of his mouth; and with the increase of his lips shall he be filled. Death and life are in the power of the tongue: and they that love it shall eat the fruit thereof."* This is talking about life like in birthing and death like in murder. It's saying that there is birthing power in the tongue and there is killing power in the tongue. In one sentence it is possible to birth something and kill something. That means I can birth prosperity and kill poverty just through my praise!

I took a hard look back in my life at all the traumatic struggles I've been through. Not the little stuff like headaches and the rent being due, but the real adversity in my life. I was thinking back to all the details that surrounded those situations. How did I come through them? How did I get past them? It was not because somebody walked in and bailed me out. Rather, I could see that it was because I decided while in that situation, that no matter what happened, no matter what was coming or what the end result was going to be, I was still going to give God praise. I was still going to live for God. I was still going to attend church. I was still going to stay in the race. I was not going to be weary in well doing, but I was going to stand when I had done all to stand. I would stay there and offer up the praises of God and when everybody else told me I ought to complain and give up, I would stand my ground, I would keep a song of praise in my heart. And I walked out of each of those situations because of that praise.

In 1 Chronicles 4:1 we learn about the product of praise through Judah and his sons. *"The sons of Judah; Pharez, Hezron, and Carmi, and Hur, and Shobal."* The name Judah means *praise*. Sometimes we can think of praise as this little euphoric thing that we get into when

• • •

we come to church, always happy with our hands up and having a good time. But you need to understand something. In that day, a child was not given a name based on "I like the sound of that; let's call him Judah!" Rather, the child was given a name based on the adversity with which that child came out of the womb at birth.

Judah did not come about by just some happy-go-lucky thing; he came out of the womb of a rejected, pushed-aside woman who was camouflaged and hidden and disguised to marry a man who didn't even want her. So Judah came forth from a situation where it wasn't easy, it wasn't fun. Momma wasn't the most popular woman on the block. The Bible said she was not desirable to look upon. She was rejected by everybody. Those are the circumstances from which Judah came forth.

If the only time you have a praise is whenever you've just walked out of something good and something blessed and something worthy of clapping your hands over, then you've got a warped reality of what praise is. You must also understand that when you praise, something is produced out of that praise. So, what does praise produce? I'm glad you asked!

Let's look at the firstborn of Judah. His name was Pharez which means *a breach, a break.* It means *a breaking forth, a gap, to cause access, to open up, to build a way, to create a path.* The first product of praise is a breakthrough! When you're in a situation where it looks like it's insurmountable and cannot be overcome, if you'll praise it will create a path through the problem that you're facing. As you praise, you're going to bust through some things that you didn't think you could ever break through. You're going to break out of some circumstances that you couldn't get yourself out of alone, all because of praise.

• • •

Judah's next son was Hezron and his name means *something prepared, a utensil, armor, artillery, carriage, furnishings, furniture, instrument, jewel that is made one of another, that which pertains to the psaltery, stuff, things, tools, vessels, weapons* and the last word is *whatsoever.* Your praise produces weapons that you put into God's hands, and as you praise Him, your weapons go to work for you. Read 2 Chronicles 20 and you will see that Jehoshophat and the children of Israel went to battle, but they did not go with swords and spears and shields. Instead they lifted up their voices and as they sang and praised God, He set ambushments to defeat the enemy that was facing their lives.

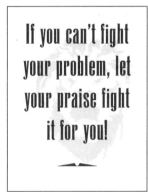

If you can't fight your problem, let your praise fight it for you!

If you can't fight your problem, let your praise fight it for you! I like it that we're talking about *whatsoever.* If you need it, whatever it is, praise will get it into your hands. If you desire peace, start praising Him. If you desire finances, start praising Him. Don't wait until the battle's over. You can…you must…praise him right now. Praise is acknowledging God for what He's done, what He's doing, and what He's going to do. So, if you've praised Him for what He's done and for what He's doing, why don't you take a little time to praise Him for what He's about to do? Yeah! That's a Hezron praise.

The next son of Judah is Carmi. Carmi means *a garden, a vineyard, vines for the production of wine or oil.* A garden is where you get your nourishment. My praise can strengthen me. Complaining and murmuring zap your strength. But your praise will birth nourishment and strength and then it's a vine that produces wine or oil. Wine removes sin; it's a symbol of blood. Oil is a symbol of anointing. It is the blood of Jesus that wiped away our sin and removed the condemnation from us, but it is the anointing of God that wipes

• • •

away the yoke and removes the burden from off of our shoulders. (Isaiah 10:27)

That tells me that when everything I'm holding onto is weighing me down, I can choose to give Him thanks, to enter into His gates with thanksgiving and into His courts with praise. I can give Him a Carmi praise that nourishes me and that lifts the burden, causing me to feel free, causing me to be loosed, causing me to walk out. Give Him a Carmi praise!

Judah (praise) gave birth to breakthrough and to weapons and to anointings. The fourth son of Judah was Hur, which means *a wall, mason, aside, a town, a shield, a protection.* When I can see my obstacle, I give Him a praise and my obstacle has to give way. And then when it gives way and I start to possess the land, oh, there are giants that I see, so I'm going to walk up in there and give Him a praise that creates a weapon. I'm going to give Him a Hezron praise. That's what I can see. Then I'm going to give Him a Carmi praise because that's what I feel. I feel heavy; I feel down; I feel unworthy; so I give Him a Carmi praise. It's easy to praise when you can see. And it's easy to praise when you feel. But a Hur praise says this, "Hey, while you're praising God, I'm going to be a wall for the things you don't see. When the enemy is trying to attack you, I'm going to stop them." They wanted to stab you in the back, but your praise created a wall. Proverbs 18:10 says, *"The name of the LORD is a strong tower: the righteous runneth into it, and is safe."*

The fourth son of Judah was Shobal and it means *overflowing.* I love that. My praise has the ability produce over…not just enough, but OVER…over. God really knows how to show up! The Bible says when Jehoshaphat and the children of Israel got there after the enemy was defeated by God, the spoils of the enemy were lying there all around. And it took them not one day, not two days, but it

• • •

took them three days to carry out all the goods! When God blesses somebody who's praising Him, you don't have arms enough to carry out all the blessing that God has for you! If you will give Him praise in all things, then you will come out of your circumstance carrying more than what you went in with in the beginning. The enemy has to bless you on your way out!

Some folks don't like a Shobal praise. They're uncomfortable around it because it's fanatical. You can't control him. You can't keep him still. He's a shouter; he's a dancer. Over in 2 Chronicles, they had trouble controlling him. He's always wanting to do something or move around or go somewhere. There's an army that rises up and Shobal praise says, "Let me go fight 'em!" All by yourself? "Yeah, yeah, by myself. I've got a prime overflowing!" He's crazy. He's out of his mind.

I began to study the Word of God and I noticed something. As David was carried into Israel and they were shouting, "Saul has slain his thousands, but David his tens of thousands…" did you know that David and the people of Israel danced before the Lord? And nobody got upset? Michel did not get upset, but the second time David came back into the city, he came in dancing and praising. The Bible says that Michel looked out of the window and despised him in her heart. The reason was, David had changed the way he praised. She was not familiar with this type of praise. What she didn't know was that David was not just coming back to Israel with the head of a giant; David was coming back with the Ark of the Covenant that had been covered with blessing. The Philistines had stacked it with diamonds and rubies and pearls and mice that were made of gold and myrrh. David was coming back into town with abundance. He was coming back into town with an overflow and it caused a praise in him that he had never had before. He kicked his shoes off and he came running in dancing and shouting and everybody was freaking out…that's a Shobal praise!

• • •

Michal told David that she couldn't believe he did this. And David replied like this, "Whoa! I've just got one thing to tell you...you ain't seen nothing yet! Tomorrow I'm going to praise Him like I haven't got a lick of sense, like I lost my mind, because I know that my Redeemer lives and I'm going to bless Him and praise Him; I'm going to magnify Him!"

Now watch this. When Michal judged David's praise, God dried up her womb. The Word said that Michal was barren from that day forward. (2 Samuel 6:14-23) If the Scripture recorded it this way, it tells me that there would have been children on the way, but God said, "You are not going to give birth if you judge another man's praise." We've learned that praise produces breakthrough, weapons, anointing, walls, and overflow. If I judge your praise, all I've done is made myself barren and I cannot produce now my own break-through, weapons, anointing, walls, and overflow.

I was talking to my dad one time and I asked him if he got everything he wanted for Christmas. He said, "Yeah, I was wanting this particular tool and I got it! But when I opened the box, it was missing the little connection to plug into the wall to charge it up, so I had to take it back." You see, you can have all the tools, but if you're not plugged in and charged up, you're not going to be effec-tive. You can know all about praise and how it works, but if you're not plugged in and praising Him, you're not going to be going any-where in your life. So, you ask, "How do I plug in?" Jesus said, *"I am the vine, you are the branches. He that abideth in me...."* (John 15:5) He has enough outlets for everybody; just plug in.

• • •

Chapter 4

I Got It in the Middle

The book of Joshua tells the story of the people of Israel after they had left their slavery in Egypt, after Moses had died on the journey, after they had spent their time in the wilderness. They were ready to go into the Promised Land. They had buried Moses and now they had to get used to following Joshua. They had to bury the old things and let new things come forth.

As we come to this story, we see that the Israelites were positioned on the brink of the Jordan, across from Jericho. The spies had spied, their report had been good, and Israel was ready to go up and take the land. But the Jordan River, high at the harvest, was between them and their goal.

Have you noticed that God just has a way of bringing us to impossible situations? It doesn't happen just so our faith can be tested, but so that we understand that God always brings us to a place where He becomes necessary in our lives. In other words, if every challenge of my life could be solved by somebody I know or by my

• • •

own doing, then there would be no need for God in my life. So He brings me to immovable objects. He brings me to uncrossable places. He brings me to unconquerable battles. Why? So that I will put my dependence and trust on Him and lean not to my own understanding. Every time God is about to do something miraculous, He puts me right in front of that impossible situation. So, Israel was standing on the bank of the Jordan River looking over at the promise.

Your greatest difficulty will always stand right in the doorway of your greatest discovery. If God is about to give you a breakthrough like you've never had before, He will lead you to a battle like you've never had before. If God is about to give you something that you've been praying and dreaming about, He will allow adversity to come before the blessing comes. The enemy wants to convince us that what stands before us is always greater than what stands after it. But, we can tell the devil that all things work together for good to them that love the Lord and who are called according to His purpose! (Romans 8:28) You will come out of your difficult situation. Whatever circumstance you find yourself in, God is able and willing to bring you out of it.

Now, it was the harvest time, and the Jordan River was at flood stage (Joshua 3:15). The people of God were standing there looking at all that water and thinking, "How in the world are we going to get over this circumstance?" But Joshua was standing there waiting for God to show up. He was looking at that river, flooded as it could be, and waiting.

Do you ever feel like that? "How can I ever get through this mess?" Just look at your Jordan! The Jordan represents an adversary; it represents roadblock; it represents impossibility; it represents struggle. The Jordan represents situations and problems in your life

• • •

that are insurmountable. It is all of those things wrapped up into one. How were all those people to get across? God gave them the answer. He said to them, "When I move, you are to follow the Ark of the Covenant wherever it goes." Isn't it something when God leads you right into an impossibility?

One reason God does this is so that when it is all over, nobody else will have gotten the praise. Anybody who becomes a creator is the one who will be worshipped. If you are a self-made man, then you will worship the one who created you. But we don't deserve the praise—God does!

The priests of God who were carrying the Ark of the Covenant started across the river, just as God had directed. They walked forth in faith into the river. And the waters stood at attention! The Bible says that the water from upstream stopped flowing and piled itself up at a town a distance away. And all the people walked across that impossible obstacle on dry ground! (Joshua 3:15-17)

In Joshua 4:4-7 we read what happened next:

Then Joshua called the twelve men, whom he had prepared of the children of Israel, out of every tribe a man: And Joshua said unto them, Pass over before the ark of the LORD your God into the midst of Jordan, and take ye up every man of you a stone upon his shoulder, according unto the number of the tribes of the children of Israel: That this may be a sign among you, that when your children ask their fathers in time to come, saying, What mean ye by these stones? Then ye shall answer them, That the waters of Jordan were cut off before the ark of the covenant of the LORD; when it passed over Jordan, the waters of Jordan were cut off: and these stones shall be for a memorial unto the children of Israel for ever.

• • •

Joshua said, "When you get in the middle of what was an impossibility, when you're standing in the middle of what was your greatest adversary, when you find yourself in the middle of what was the greatest struggle in your life…I want you to reach down and grab a stone from the middle of your adversity. That stone was down underneath there all the time!" The stones that these men were to pick up were already there under the river. There's always something of value that lies beneath your problem and your struggle. You are to find out what it is.

> There's always something of value that lies beneath your problem and your struggle.

And Joshua said, "Pick that stone up and put it on your shoulders so we can carry it out of this situation. It is to be for a memorial." The word *memorial* signifies a legacy that provokes remembrance and thanksgiving. A memorial should energize you and evoke a praise. When I look at a memorial for those who died in times of war, I am grateful and I am thankful that somebody put their life on the line so that we could enjoy the freedom that we have today. Though you yourself may never have seen war, somebody fought and died on your behalf. That knowledge provokes thanksgiving in you. It produces praise in you. It provokes a benefit that is remembered through your thanksgiving.

Joshua here is saying, "I want you to know that when you get in the middle of that circumstance you thought you'd never get out of, that you thought you'd never get rid of, would never cross through, never make it over, something is waiting for you there. When you get to the middle of your circumstance, there is a praise waiting for you!"

• • •

When you find yourself slap dab in the middle of your difficult situation, you are to pick up your tambourine, pick up your praise, pick up your song to the Lord! You don't have to wait until you get out of your problems. You've got to praise Him while you're in the middle of it and let God turn your circumstances around.

I've found out that I dictate when God shows up. You don't believe me? Well, you determine when God shows up, too! If you wait to praise Him until after the battle's over, He'll only show up when it's over. Psalm 22:3 tells us that He inhabits the praises of His people. So, if you'll praise Him while you're in the middle of it, God will show up there! Don't wait until the battle is over; lift up a praise in the middle of it! No matter what you're going through, God will show up—in your finances, in your relationships, in your body, in your mind. He's showing up every time you give Him a praise, every time you say, *"Bless the Lord, O my soul; and all that is within me, bless His holy name!"* (Psalm 103:1) We've got to praise Him in the middle!

When we praise God in the middle of our adversity, we can say, "Hallelujah! I got it in the middle! I'm not waiting…I want out of this trial! I'm walking through the valley, but I've got a praise on my lips! I'm coming out! I am blessed!"

It's so easy to let your praise be covered up by all the adversity around you when you're standing there in the middle of your situation. Your praise becomes covered over with your problems. But, there's a praise somewhere down there. Why didn't God let the people ride a boat across that river? Because the praise was at the bottom of it! God may let you hit the bottom if it's the only way to get His praise out of your life. And so they got to the middle, and they picked up these large rocks. The rocks had two purposes: It's a reminder for you, and it's a testimony to your children.

• • •

We have to understand that our complaining at home will affect our children. If you say, "Woe is me. Everybody's always picking on me. Why do I have to go through this struggle?" then you have to realize that your children are feeling the effects of your doubt and unbelief, your low-talking and low-walking attitude. What are they hearing? "We'll never make it out. We'll never see the daylight after this darkness. We'll never make enough money to make it." How do you know God isn't going to have somebody deliver you of all your debt with one check? How do you know what God will or will not do?

When you get in the middle, pick up a praise. There's nothing like a middle-of-the-mess-praise! You're no praiser if you can't praise Him in the middle of your mess! You aren't a praiser if the sun's got to be shining and your bank account's got to be full of money before you'll praise the Lord.

And the people came up out of Jordan on the tenth day of the first month, and encamped in Gilgal, in the east border of Jericho. And those twelve stones, which they took out of Jordan, did Joshua pitch in Gilgal." (Joshua 4:19-20)

"And the people came up out…" A praise always brings you, not just out, but up out. You can come out at the same level you went in, but a praise has a way of bringing you *up* out. I don't know about you, but I don't want to just come out. I want to be at another level when I do come out. I want to look at the devil and say, "Listen! I want my stuff back!" I want a pressed-down-shaken-together miracle!

Let's look at something else of interest in this story of Israel. God had told the people to follow the Ark. So they followed it, and they came to the Jordan. You see, the Ark led them to the Jordan where the adversity was, where the obstacle was. And then God told them to get their praise out from the middle of that situation. Remember they were

• • •

headed for Gilgal and they were following God. They didn't arrive at Gilgal on their own. *"The steps of a good man are ordered by the Lord."* (Psalm 37:23) They were following God UP out of this.

Once they got to the other side, we see in Joshua 4:19-20 that they camped at Gilgal and they placed the stones from the midst of the Jordan there. What I want you to see is that they got their praise IN their circumstance which propelled them to go UP out of their circumstance and they pitched their praise in Gilgal.

The name Gilgal means *wheel*. A wheel turns. So if I will get my praise while I'm in the midst of my circumstance, my praise will lead me to a place where my situation becomes totally turned around. Did you ever need something turned around that you didn't want to wait six weeks for? You didn't want to wait half a year...or a year? Just go ahead and give Him all the praise, and while you're praising, He starts turning your situation around. He starts turning people's hearts toward you. While you bless Him, He starts turning doctor's opinions about you. Praise Him in the middle and watch God turn it around.

Look at Paul and Silas in Acts 16:25-26. At midnight...that's the middle of the situation. Paul and Silas were in prison, strapped to the walls. And Paul said, "Silas, do you have a key to this thing?" And Silas said, "No, I don't, but I think I can get one out of my mouth and if we'll start praisin' Him..." It was midnight, in the middle of their dark circumstances, that Paul and Silas began to bless the Lord. All of a sudden their jail started shaking! The foundation of *your* problem is waiting on you to make a decision! Will you praise God in the middle?

Back to Joshua and the children of Israel. They praised Him and God turned it around! What did He turn? Joshua 5:1 tells us:

> *And it came to pass, when all the kings of the Amorites, which were on the side of Jordan westward, and all the kings of the*

• • •

Canaanites, which were by the sea, heard that the LORD had dried up the waters of Jordan from before the children of Israel, until we were passed over, that their heart melted, neither was there spirit in them any more, because of the children of Israel.

Hey, look! No swords, no spears. They were coming out of the desert with just buckets to hold manna. They had been in bondage four hundred years and in the desert forty more and they haven't fought a battle yet! How can their enemy possibly be scared of a people like that, of a people with no weapons? The answer is awesome! It's because the weapons of our warfare are not carnal (2 Corinthians 10:4) and when your enemy watches your praise while you're in the middle of any impossibility, it messes with his head! He's thinking, "These are crazy folks here! They're going through it. They don't have a thing. They look like they're about to die. They've been wearing the same shoes for forty years; they don't have weapon one, no horses or chariots. And here they come running up against us singing! What is that they're singing?"

Oh, let me tell you, they're singing "Blessed be the name of the Lord God of Israel for he hath thrown the horse and rider into the sea! The same thing He did to Pharoah, He's going to do to you!" That's what they're singing.

Read Joshua 5:10-12 and follow on with the story.

And the children of Israel encamped in Gilgal, and kept the passover on the fourteenth day of the month at even in the plains of Jericho. And they did eat of the old corn of the land on the morrow after the passover, unleavened cakes, and parched corn in the selfsame day. And the manna ceased on the morrow after they had eaten of the old corn of the land; neither had the children of Israel manna any more; but they did eat of the fruit of the land of Canaan that year.

• • •

God is a turn-it-around-in-a-day God. For so long in the wilderness Israel had been used to getting their supply day by day. Every day manna came; the next day manna came. God didn't let them store it up from the day before; it would rot. They couldn't store it, so He brought them fresh manna every day.

Now look at this and get this! God leads them to an impossible situation. They get into the middle of it and He says, If you'll praise Me while you're in the middle, I'll lead you to a place of turnaround, and I'll take you from a place of daily provision to a place of yearly provision." God was saying that what used to take a year for you to make, if you'll praise Him while you're in the middle, He'll turn that situation around and give you in a day what it took you a year to get.

God's agenda is always to show up in the middle. He desires to be in the middle. Whatever is in the middle is what you hang things on to keep balance. Think of Jesus. I don't know the thief on the left, and the thief on the right deserves what he's getting, but this One Who's in the middle…why is He there? He's always in the middle. If He'd been put on the left or on the right, He couldn't have reached both. But He's right in the middle, reaching for all men.

Praise Him while you're in the middle of it. Don't let your circumstances steal your praise! Bless the Lord. I want God to turn my situation around! Yes, right there in the middle of the circumstances that are bigger than you, shout "Hallelujah! Praise You Lord!" He wants to be right there in the middle with you!

• • •

• • •

Chapter 5

Sound Advice

I've bought a lot of cars and trucks in my life. I don't keep vehicles long. I like to keep them about two years and then trade them in. Some time back, my brother and I went truck shopping for him. So we go out and start looking around. The way we shopped for a truck was to get in first. Climb in and get comfortable. Check out the seats, you know. Then you turn the radio on! That's important! The sound is important! When I go check out a vehicle, I never lift the hood, but I want to make sure the sound system is right. I'm not so interested in what size the engine is or the horsepower rating, whether it's a V-8 or V-12 or whatever. I don't know. I thought a V-8 was a drink, but anyway…. You don't worry about it. But you want to hear if the sound works all right. Now I'm to the point where I don't really even care what it sounds like, because before I even buy, I know that I'll take it straight to the car stereo shop and have them redo my sound. You know, I like some subs and all that stuff up in my vehicle.

• • •

When you're looking at different makes and models of vehicles, it's funny how the sounds are different. You climb into a truck and turn the radio on and they're all set to a country station. You have to find the station you want to see if it's going to handle your style, but in a truck dealership, they're going to have it on country stations. But, you go to a Mercedes dealership and you sit in an S55 four-door, stretched out and you turn the radio on and it's smooth jazz. Everything's smooth and nice. The other day I saw a 1978

> Sound has a powerful way of increasing depression or increasing joy.

Impala. It was worth, like three thousand dollars. The sound system in it was worth about thirteen thousand dollars! Why is that? It's because sound can match and dictate an environment.

Scientists study light and sound and the elements that we cannot touch, but yet experience. The wind cannot be seen, for example, but the effects of it can be seen. Sound cannot be captured in a box, yet we can turn on a box and hear sound. It's amazing what sound can do. Sound sets the atmosphere. Sound changes mentality and sound can change the entire atmosphere around you. Sound has a powerful way of increasing depression or increasing joy. It can remind you of a bad past or it can remind you of a good time in the past. It can bring you up or bring you down. Sound can scare you. It can shock you. Sound can soothe you, put you to sleep. Sound can make you nervous. And sound can make you calm. It's amazing, the art of sound.

You can go to certain places and the sound you here will be a reminder. The music in the elevator is picked out to be soothing and light, not sinister, while you're riding in there sixty stories up! When you go to the dentist's office and are sitting there waiting for your turn. Did you notice that they're not playing hard rock music? No, they want you to calm down! How about the doctor's office? They already know you're nervous and a little upset. You don't know what's getting ready to be said to you, so they calm you with the music.

In light of all this, pay attention to this verse of Scripture.

But I say, Have they not heard? Yes verily, **their sound** *went into all the earth, and* **their words** *unto the ends of* **the world**. (Romans 10:18, emphasis added)

Then let's look back into the Old Testament for another verse.

And Hannah prayed, and said, My heart rejoiceth in the LORD, mine horn is exalted in the LORD: **my mouth is enlarged over mine enemies;** *because I rejoice in thy salvation.* (1 Samuel 2:1, emphasis added)

Sound sets a pace. Look at Psalm 150. David says to praise Him with the sound of trumpets. Trumpets indicate the entrance of royalty, or the advancement and the uniting for war. David is saying that when you get in the service, understand that there is a temperature that is going to come into that service. And when you begin to thank God, when you begin to bless God in the firmament of His power, and you begin to express to Him who He is in His mighty greatness, then you need to understand that the first thing we are going to set in the atmosphere is trumpets. They dictate His arrival into your praise.

The next thing he says is to praise Him with the psaltery and harp. That's the stringed instruments. When you play the strings, it brings a different dynamic. They set the atmosphere of worship, of adoration. You understand that in His presence all of a sudden you become like Mary where you fall to your knees. And everything you value, you offer to Him, including yourself. And you pour your worship out on Him. Maybe others are saying things about you and talking bad about you. But in the middle of worship, all of a sudden, He just brushes

• • •

your hair back and lets you know that everything is going to be all right. No matter what anybody may say or do, it is in His presence that we understand we are washed clean, and we are made to be like Him.

After the worshipping strings, the next instrument of praise is the loud cymbals. Cymbals represent victory. When you hear cymbals, you're hearing the sound of victory. Look at 2 Chronicles 5:13. In this passage, when they praised just like this, all their praise came up together and joined in to make ONE sound. At that moment, the glory of God filled the house where they were sitting!

> If you want to change where you are going, you've got to change your sound.

You must understand the power of sound. The type of sound that comes together indicates and directs a specific direction. Sound determines direction. Sound indicates where something is headed. Everything that exists today is matched in power by sound. A baby's cry indicates that it is a small infant child. A warrior's cry identifies that we have a giant in our midst. Sound brings with it significant impact.

I remember when I was a little boy we used to go to a church that was about a mile and half from a railroad track. You could hear the train, but you couldn't see it. By hearing it, though, you knew it was a train. The significance of that piece of equipment was accompanied by the significance of its sound. They came together. And even though you couldn't see it, you still new it was a train. The train and its sound were a powerful force that flowed together.

Sound will identify to us exactly where we are going, but it will also identify to us where we've been. If you want to change where you are going, you've got to change your sound. Sometimes you don't need anybody to say even one word for you to be able to identify their sound. Think about that. If I were to play one of your favorite songs for you right now, you'd recognize who it is before they ever sang the first note. Why? Because they have their own sound. And you recognize them by that sound. Musical genius understands that players sometimes change. Singers and musicians come and go. But if you keep the same sound, folks have the same reaction. A band or group can go through four or five new members and nobody cares as long as they have the some sound.

Sound tells you where you're going. Nobody has to say a word. You can hear a sound and it will identify what's coming afterwards. In other words, the Bible says that David played upon his harp and then Saul was delivered from the evil spirit that was upon him. (1 Samuel 16:23.) Jehoshaphat began to praise God and sing praises in the face of the enemy. And the Bible says that God set ambushments against his enemy. (2 Chronicles 20:20-25.) Read in Acts chapter 16 where Paul and Silas began to pray and sing praises, and the jail was shaken and everybody there understood that freedom was coming. Why? Because your sound will always be before your deliverance. If you want to get free, you have to learn how to make the right sound. If you want freedom, shout for freedom. If you want deliverance, praise Him to deliverance. If you want to turn around, give Him glory and you'll see a turnaround.

In I Samuel 2:1 we read that Hannah came to the tabernacle. Hannah was barren, without the ability to produce a child. The Scripture records that she knew who the priest was and that the priest was familiar with her, too. He called her by name. This time Hannah got there and she got there fed up with getting the "same old same old." Hannah did not change churches to get her deliverance.

• • •

Hannah didn't change pastors to get her deliverance. What did Hannah do? She changed her sound. The Scripture indicates that when the priest heard her this time, he thought she was drunk out of her mind. He had never seen or heard her acting this way before.

If you have decided that you've had enough, you can change your circumstances just by changing your sound. Sound tells me what's about to happen. If you want to know what your future holds, it is going to be identified by the present sound. If you have a complaining depressing sound in your present, you don't need to call any psychic to see what's coming. You don't need to get in any prophet's line for him to tell you what's getting ready to happen. Close your eyes and get ready for a depressing, complaining, low, empty future…based on your present sound. But if you decide that you're tired of having a low down, depressed present and you've looked in your past and it hasn't been what you wanted it to be, you can then release a new sound that says, "I don't have to SEE victory; I'm just going to sing it UNTIL I see it come into my life!"

Have you ever talked with someone who has survived a hurricane? What do they say? "Did you see it?"

"No, I didn't see it."

"Did you know it was coming?"

"Oh, I knew it was coming."

"How did you know it was coming?"

"It sounded like a train."

What are you telling me? A powerful force is accompanied by a powerful sound. And the sound will tell you what's on the way. If you'll wake up every morning of your life and start giving God the

• • •

praise, I guarantee you that you're going to see a victorious day somewhere in your future. You need to change your sound!

Look again in Romans 10:18. Their words—the sound that comes out of them— will last until the end. Be cautious that you don't expend judgment rather than grace. Because whatever comes out of our mouth goes into your future, not your past! You don't speak toward your past; you speak toward your future. It goes forward, and your sound will tell you what's coming next. It amazes me how many of us can quote the verse before this one. Verse 17 says, *"So then faith cometh by hearing, and hearing by the Word of God."* But the next verse says that we need to know that our sound goes into all the earth and our words to the end.

Your sound will tell you what is to follow. In the Scriptures, God is portrayed as a father. If a son were to ask the father for a piece of bread, would he give him a stone? Would he give him a snake? No, He would not treat His son any differently than you would yours. I have two children and I would never try to harm them through what they ask of me. I wouldn't give them poison if they asked for a drink or something to eat. I give them what they need, how they need it.

Now, God is just like a regular dad. So, if God is like me, I'm sitting in my living room watching television. If I hear my children playing and if I hear them carrying on just like they do every day of their lives, I don't worry about what's going on because I'm accustomed to their sound. But, if all of a sudden I hear my child's voice make a different sound than what I'm accustomed to, something on the inside of me rises up. I don't care what I may be doing, when I hear my child I abandon my present occupation to find my child and to rescue my child, not based on what I saw, but just based on what I heard.

• • •

The problem is that most of us let distance get between God and ourselves. The only time God hears us is when we have trouble. God starts coming to us but keeps getting delayed by fold that are with Him. See, He was going to the little girl at Jairus' house, but got stopped three times by folk that were with Him. So, the thing is, how do I keep from drifting so far away from God that now I have to shout in fear to get His attention. I'm glad you asked. The Bible says that God inhabits the sound of your heart and gratitude.

Praise is not an intention of the heart or a meditation of the mind. Praise is, *"Let every thing that hath breath praise the Lord!"* (Psalm 150:6) The original translation says, "Let anybody breathing make the sound of gratitude to be heard." When God hears the sound of gratitude coming out of my mouth, He doesn't let me go anywhere without Him with me. Every day of my life I praise Him so we can walk together through situations and storms of life. I know that He's with me and He'll never leave me or forsake me because as long as I have breath, the sound of praise will never leave my mouth. And He will never leave my side. The only time He lets go is to get in front of me and make a way where there seems to be no way. And to tear down walls that are in front of me. Then He takes my hand and leads me into the promise that He provided.

You need to change your sound. If you want out of your circumstance, just start praising Him. Give Him thanks; give Him glory.

Chapter 6

Behind the Music

In 1993 I drove to Orlando with my family to start this church. I had never been in the city limits of Orlando in my life. Didn't know a person. Didn't know a bank. Didn't know where to rent a house. I drove in with nothing but my family and my calling.

My only experience in the Orlando community in my life happened two years earlier when I stood on this platform with Rod Parsley and sang, *There's a Healer in the House.* And this church is not within the city limits. I was just a music boy, but something lay behind.... Everybody said, "That's Rod Parsley's music director." But God said, "No, that's your future pastor." He allowed me to see where I would eventually have authority. Why? Because something was there behind the music.

Everybody has gifts and callings, abilities and talents. And there's always a story that lies behind those talents, the gifts and the abilities that you have. There are always experiences, always things

• • •

that you have done, things you have accomplished in life and things you have gone through in life to get to the place where you are now. There are some people who haven't been through a great lot of things. Those folks just don't have as many testimonies! But there are some people who have been through some troubling times in life, some times that pushed you past the limits of what you thought you could survive. And you can testify boldly that "can't nobody do me like Jesus!"

We must look at what lies behind the music, behind the callings, talents, gifts, and abilities. Saul and David are perfect examples to turn to in order to see what truly lies behind. We can learn what not to do from Saul's side of the story and we can learn how to build character behind our gifts and talents from David. Let's begin with Saul.

> *But the Spirit of the LORD departed from Saul, and an evil spirit from the LORD troubled him. And Saul's servants said unto him, Behold now, an evil spirit from God troubleth thee. Let our lord now command thy servants, which are before thee, to seek out a man, who is a cunning player on an harp: and it shall come to pass, when the evil spirit from God is upon thee, that he shall play with his hand, and thou shalt be well. And Saul said unto his servants, Provide me now a man that can play well, and bring him to me. Then answered one of the servants, and said, Behold, I have seen a son of Jesse the Bethlehemite, that is cunning in playing, and a mighty valiant man, and a man of war, and prudent in matters, and a comely person, and the LORD is with him. Wherefore Saul sent messengers unto Jesse, and said, Send me David thy son, which is with the sheep.* (1 Samuel 16:14-19)

• • •

David was a young man that few people saw much potential in, but God saw beyond the outer appearance of what others saw. Samuel went to the house of Jesse and totally missed the one God sent him there to anoint because he judged everything by what was on the outside. But don't you know that in David, something lay behind the music! His brothers just saw him as a little harp player in the mountain. His daddy thought he was just a little songwriter that sat up there with the sheep. But God saw something behind the music. Everybody just saw a little shepherd boy and a psalmist, but God said there was a king up under all that stuff that everybody else saw!

Look at 1 Samuel 16:11-12:

And Samuel said unto Jesse, Are here all thy children? And he said, There remaineth yet the youngest, and, behold, he keepeth the sheep. And Samuel said unto Jesse, Send and fetch him: for we will not sit down till he come hither. And he sent, and brought him in. Now he was ruddy, and withal of a beautiful countenance, and goodly to look to. And the LORD said, Arise, anoint him: for this is he.

Notice, all of the sons were part of the house, but the one that was promoted was the only one that smelled like sheep. All the boys were part of Jesse's house, but only one of them smelled like sheep. Can I just tell you that you will never be promoted in the Kingdom if you don't know how to serve in an area in the house where you smell like sheep when you're finished? You have to realize that God is truly searching for those who smell like sheep. All of these other guys had it all together, but there was one boy, when he came in, he didn't smell like everybody else. He smelled like sheep. He didn't mind getting involved with sheep. He didn't mind rubbing shoulders with stuff that everybody else wanted to abandon and get away from.

• • •

The Bible tells us that Saul reached a point in his life where an evil spirit tormented him and would not give him rest or peace. This didn't just come upon him one day. There were reasons for this. Read what the Word says here:

> *And Samuel came to Saul: and Saul said unto him, Blessed be thou of the LORD: I have performed the commandment of the LORD. And Samuel said, What meaneth then this bleating of the sheep in mine ears, and the lowing of the oxen which I hear? And Saul said, They have brought them from the Amalekites: for the people spared the best of the sheep and of the oxen, to sacrifice unto the LORD thy God; and the rest we have utterly destroyed. Then Samuel said unto Saul, Stay, and I will tell thee what the LORD hath said to me this night. And he said unto him, Say on. And Samuel said, When thou wast little in thine own sight, wast thou not made the head of the tribes of Israel, and the LORD anointed thee king over Israel?* (1 Samuel 15:13-17)

In other words, the first thing Saul lost was his ability to stay humble. You're about to lose your authority if you ever rise above the fact that you don't remember where you've been, where you've come from, and who you really are. You're about to lose your title. God's about to strip you of something. You're about to lose your level in ministry the moment you forget where you've come from.

> *And the LORD sent thee on a journey, and said, Go and utterly destroy the sinners the Amalekites, and fight against them until they be consumed. Wherefore then didst thou not obey the voice of the LORD, but didst fly upon the spoil, and didst evil in the sight of the LORD?* (1 Samuel 15:18-19)

The second place where Saul messed up was by his refusal to obey the voice of the Lord. If God tells you to do something, you better do it! I'm not talking about when somebody grabs you and

• • •

prophesies over you, but I'm talking about when you know God told you to do something and you're still not doing it. I'm talking about the Word of God and the voice of God in your life. I'm talking to folks who don't tithe. I'm talking to people who don't get involved. They just come and take without giving, without imparting to others. God told Saul to do something and Saul refused to do it. He refused to remain humble, and he refused to obey the voice of God.

> It's time for the body of Christ to realize that you can't advance yourself without living in a state of humility, understanding "to prefer."

Now read the next couple of verses.

> *And Saul said unto Samuel, Yea, I have obeyed the voice of the LORD, and have gone the way which the LORD sent me, and have brought Agag the king of Amalek, and have utterly destroyed the Amalekites. But the people took of the spoil, sheep and oxen, the chief of the things which should have been utterly destroyed, to sacrifice unto the LORD thy God in Gilgal.* (1 Samuel 15:20-21)

The third thing Saul did was refuse to take responsibility for his own actions. He refused. It's vital that you understand this. What is needed for your elevation and your advancement is what lies behind your talent and your ability. And the first thing you need behind there is your ability to walk in humility. I don't care how well you can sing. I don't care how well you can play. I don't care how well you have crafted your gift. You've got to remain humble because it is the humble that God shall exalt. (Matthew 23:12) It's time for the body of Christ to realize that you can't advance yourself without living in

• • •

a state of humility, understanding "to prefer." John the Baptist said this, *"He must increase, but I must decrease."* (John 3:30)

So Saul has been stripped of his authority and his anointing. And David has been given the authority and the anointing. And this is when the Scripture tells us that an evil spirit came upon Saul. (1 Samuel 16:14) He's frustrated. He's aggravated. He's mad. He can't find peace. He can't get any rest. Watch what Saul said when the anointing lifted. *"Bring me a man that is skillful, or cunning, in his playing."* (1 Samuel 16:17) Did you catch the mistake Saul made here? He thought he could replace the anointing with ability. He didn't ask for somebody anointed; he asked for somebody with ability. That's how a lot of churches mess up whenever pastors look for music directors who have a lot of ability but fall way short on anointing. There better be something behind that ability that is called anointing. You can't replace the anointing with just ability.

I had a musician one time when I was a music director. He came to me at the end of a service and said, "I want to apologize because I only gave God fifty percent tonight. I had my mind on other things and my heart in other places. So I want to apologize to you and, if you give me the opportunity, I'll apologize to the choir and the band because I didn't come up here prepared. And I didn't give God my hundred percent tonight."

I said, "All right. That's fine." So he stood in front of the choir and the band and he apologized. When he was finished, everybody gave him an applause and all that. And I said, "That's all fine and everything and we appreciate you humbling yourself to do that. But I want everybody to learn a lesson here with this because you all need to understand. This man did not give God fifty percent. He didn't give God anything."

• • •

About that time, they all kind of looked at me like *what is he talkin' about!* I said, "He only *offered* God fifty percent." We don't give God our praise. We offer God the sacrifice of our praise. And we found out in Genesis that God doesn't take every offering that He's given. Cain found out that you don't give God anything. Everything is an offering. Everything is a sacrifice and God will determine what He receives and what He takes.

The truth is, you haven't given God anything until you've learned how to bless Him when the sun isn't shining, when the rain's falling, and when you don't have a reason to say, "Hallelujah," but you've still got a praise anyway. You don't have a reason to clap your hands, but you clap them anyway. You don't have a reason to shout with a voice of triumph, but you push through your struggle and through your problems and say, "Hey! I'm still going to bless Him at all times!" You need to learn how to give Him a sacrifice.

Now, let's take a look at David, the one whom the servant sent to Saul.

> *Then answered one of the servants, and said, Behold, I have seen a son of Jesse the Bethlehemite, that is cunning in playing, and a mighty valiant man, and a man of war, and prudent in matters, and a comely person, and the LORD is with him.*
> (1 Samuel 16:18)

His servant, in essence, was telling Saul, "Hey, I found somebody who's skillful, but there's something that rests behind the music."

This passage tells us that there are five characteristics behind the music of David's life. The Word says that he was cunning in his playing. That's the first thing behind David; he perfected his gift. Now, I can get upset when someone comes to church and

• • •

they want to rely on just the anointing. I can hear you right now. "Well, you just said you had to have that anointing…" Yes, but I didn't say anointing alone was everything. I said your ability is nothing without anointing. But I didn't say you had everything when you just have the anointing. I've seen a lot of folks with a lot of ability who didn't have any anointing. But I've not seen many folks who were really anointed who had not perfected their abili-

> **I've seen a lot of folks with a lot of ability who didn't have any anointing.**

ties. You can pray all day long, but if you don't practice, you're going to get up there and be a bad representative of the Kingdom of God. And you're going to give someone an earache! They'll choose to run to the restroom every time you are introduced to sing!

Whatever gifting God has given you…and I'm not just talking about singing and playing music; I'm talking about the gifts that lie in your life that God has given you; it is your responsibility to perfect them, just like David.

Not only had David perfected his gift, but he was a valiant man. That word *valiant* means *to fear nothing*. Second Timothy 1:7 says, *"For God hath not given us the spirit of fear, but of power, and of love, and of a sound mind."* Beneath the surface of your life there needs to lie a fight in you, a determination to be a success regardless of what obstacles come your way. You must not fear what the enemy may have devised for you. How many people want to be a millionaire? Then you'd better learn how to risk some things. You'd better learn how to step on some stuff nobody else wants to step on. You'd better be ready to get out of that boat when all the other disciples want to stay in it! If you keep your eyes on Jesus like Peter did, you can walk where natural men sink.

• • •

Think about David. He was sixteen years old and some man was pouring anointing oil on him saying, "You're about to lead the nation of Israel." David had to accept that responsibility. He had to be fearless. That's why he could walk in the midst of Goliath, in the shadow of the giant and say, "I will fear no evil: for thou art with me, thy rod and thy staff they comfort me." (Psalm 23:4)

The Scripture also tells us that David was *a man of war.* He was a fighter! Listen, anybody who will walk up to a sword-wielding giant and just have a sling shot in his hand, that guy's got something in his gut! And it's not fear! And that day David looked that giant in the eye and said, "Let me tell you something! This day I'm going to feed your carcass to the birds of the air!" (1 Samuel 17:45-46.) That's fearless! (Zechariah 4:6) "Oh, but David, that giant's too big to beat!" And David's reply, "No, He's too big to miss!"

You'd better know you're in a fight when the devil comes like a lion and steals something. David saw a lion and said, "Oh no! You're not takin' that from me!" Saul asked David how he was going to face this Goliath. And David responded, "I fought a lion. I fought a bear. And the same God who delivered me out of the paw of the lion and the bear will deliver me from this uncircumcised Philistine!"

What else does this passage tell us about David? David was *prudent in his manners.* Uh-oh, we might have just eliminated a whole big bunch of folks there! Let me put that in plain English. He is on time with his bills. David was a man of character. "Well," you say, "I have the Holy Ghost." Well, do you pay your bills? Have your lights been cut off three times this month? "Well, that's just an attack from the devil. He's trying to get me." Yeah. The power company is the one after you. They have Ouija boards and all kinds of stuff up there, and they're led by an evil spirit to find your house. I mean, they drive by and they say, "There it is! Willie, we're going to

• • •

cut off their electricity because of the shekinah glory hovering over that house over there! That's it Willie! We're turning that one off!" No, that's not an attack from the devil, my friend. They're just going down through the bills and seeing your name and the bill not paid.

The next thing our Scripture says was behind David's gift is this: He was *a comely person.* He was humble. He was not prideful. Humility precedes recovery. If you want to get anything back that the enemy stole, do it through humility. *"If my people, which are called by my name, shall humble themselves, and pray, and seek my face, and turn from their wicked ways; then will I hear from heaven, and will forgive their sin, and will heal their land."* (2 Chronicles 7:14) He's not talking to the world here. "If My people shall humble themselves..." The first step to recovery. Later He says, "I'll hear from heaven. I'll heal your land. I'll fix what's wrong, but only when you walk in humility." Humility precedes recovery.

The final truth revealed to us about David in our text is that *the Lord is with him.* Do you understand that if God is with you, that favor is with you? If God is with you, then power is with you. Behind your gifts and your abilities there had better lie an understanding that you cannot make it without God being with you. I've come to find out that if I've got Him, I am the majority!

Did you notice that Saul sent to Jesse's house and told him to send David to him? God opens doors of opportunity. If you will perfect what you have, and if you will be fearless, and if you will be a bold fighter, if you will be prudent in all your matters, if you will stay humble before God, and if you will walk knowing you can't live without Him with you, He will open doors for you. David was getting an invitation to where he was going to eventually live.

Yes, God has a way! When you don't think it will ever happen for you, don't ever underestimate God. If there's stuff behind your

• • •

abilities, your day is coming! You may have been picked over by everybody else and misidentified by even prophetic gifts. But God doesn't miss anybody! Samuel tried to anoint Jesse's other boys, but your oil won't flow on anybody else's head. Your oil. And nobody else can take what God has destined for you!

• • •

Chapter 7

Mouth Alert!

I grew up in the Deep South. We had to pump sunshine where we lived. We didn't have enough money to pay attention. My daddy used to always laugh at me because I would continually talk about what I was going to have and where I was going to be and what I was going to do and what I was going to possess. You have to realize, this wasn't when I was twenty years old. No, I was ten years old going around talking like that! That kind of talk was coming up from deep inside of me.

Most every testimony was something like, "Y'all pray for me that I'll hold on. I've just barely made it this week. Oh God, if You knew what I was going through!" Truth was, we *all* knew what she was going through because she told everybody at the beauty shop. She told everybody at the grocery store. She told everybody sitting in the living room drinking coffee. Everybody knew what she was going through!

But I used to say, "This is not where I'm going to end up." It wasn't the geography I was talking about either. I was talking about

• • •

a mindset, a mentality. I was determined that I was not going to live my life griping, complaining, lying around, waiting for God to take me home, barely hanging on…. No, not me! I decided way back then that I wasn't just barely hanging on; I was climbing the rope! I decided I was going to ring the bell; I was getting to the top.

What comes out of our mouths is incredibly important. Our talk shapes our walk. There are some vital things about your mouth that I

Your miracle starts with your mouth.

want you to learn here. In Matthew 21:16 we read, *"Hearest thou what these say? And Jesus saith unto them, Yea; have ye never read, Out of the mouth of babes and sucklings thou hast perfected praise?"* God is a unique character. Everything that God created with the exception of man was created through the spoken word. The same spirit that raised Christ from the dead now dwells in us empowering us to walk in authority and do the things God has given us to do. God has handed down to us everything He has. His authority belongs to you. His power belongs to you. His dominion belongs to you. You need to understand that you are not a wimp today! You have God's authority.

If you will learn about your mouth and put that knowledge into practice, God wants to lay a foundation under you. Your miracle starts with your mouth. It doesn't start with your pocketbook. Have you ever said, "Oh, if I just had enough money…."? But it's not about the money. A mouth can move a mountain. (Mark 11:23) If you will learn how to use what God has given you, you can walk in complete victory.

You're going to see how important a mouth alert is. There are some people around who just seem to live to complain. That's all they ever do. Their talk and their lives are filled with misery, agony, bad luck, and depression. I don't live by luck, though. I live by

• • •

divine purpose. If a storm is coming my way, obviously it's there to blow me in the right direction, not to blow me over, but to change my direction. See, you can utilize anything. The old preacher said, "If somebody throws you a lemon, make lemonade out of it." Don't worry about it. One time a man gave me a car. It was a piece of junk really. I had a choice. I could sit there and say, "Well, dear Lord, this is a piece of junk." Or I could say, "Wow! This is great! Yesterday I didn't have a car at all and today I have one! It sure beats walking! Thank you! Praise God!" I chose the latter and was happy. Before long I put a good two-hundred-dollar paint job on it. Then I got some Mag wheels put on it, an eight-track player.... Oops, excuse me! Dating myself, huh! I let that old junk car be a blessing and a direction-setter in my life rather than a place to fall down and complain. And I moved forward in joy.

Even so the tongue is a little member, and boasteth great things. Behold, how great a matter a little fire kindleth! And the tongue is a fire, a world of iniquity: so is the tongue among our members, that it defileth the whole body, and setteth on fire the course of nature; and it is set on fire of hell. For every kind of beasts, and of birds, and of serpents, and of things in the sea, is tamed, and hath been tamed of mankind: But the tongue can no man tame; it is an unruly evil, full of deadly poison. Therewith bless we God, even the Father; and therewith curse we men, which are made after the similitude of God. Out of the same mouth proceedeth blessing and cursing. My brethren, these things ought not so to be. Doth a fountain send forth at the same place sweet water and bitter? Can the fig tree, my brethren, bear olive berries? either a vine, figs? so can no fountain both yield salt water and fresh. (James 3:5-12)

That's a lot to write about such a little thing as a tongue—your mouth. A bonfire is touched off by a little fire, a little spark. Can

you think back to times when bonfires got set off in your relationships or finances or emotions because of the little fire we call your tongue? Sometimes those raging fires can grow out of something as simple as a word spoken in jest. A jest can be packed with a lot of truth. That can get you into trouble, too! James in this Scripture tells us that a fountain does not send forth bitter water and sweet water at the same time. What about our tongue?

Have you ever been to the circus? Remember seeing those ferocious lions. You could just feel how powerful and strong they were. Do you think they were tame? If they were, then why do you suppose they would put tame animals into those big massive cages? The answer is simple. That lion is not really tame. He's been trained. James tells us that no one can tame the tongue. He says it's unruly, it's poison. The tongue, indeed, cannot be tamed, but it can be trained to say those things that will promote God's involvement in your life. God steps in when everyone else steps out. We gain His involvement through training our tongue.

Can you see the deep importance of learning how to train your mouth? You must realize when you open your mouth and speak, you are not just affecting yourself. Everybody around you is affected by what you say and how you speak. If you don't believe that's true, just let me hang around your children for a little while, and I can tell you everything going on at your house!

Look with me at Isaiah 50:4. *"The Lord GOD hath given me the tongue of the learned, that I should know how to speak a word in season to him that is weary...."* In 1 Corinthians 2:4 Paul tells us that his speech and his preaching was not with enticing words of man's wisdom, yet the Bible tells us to speak as wise men. Paul is saying, "I don't know how to say it to impress you, but I know what to say to affect you."

• • •

It's important for you to realize how powerful and influential your words are. When you're at work and doing your job, your words affect people around you. There are too many people who go to work Monday morning and they murmur and complain. They grumble about how the service went til two o'clock. Man, I didn't get my nap. It was so cotton-pickin' hot in there I thought I was in the jungle with no air. That sound system was up so loud my ears were bleeding before I could get out of there. Then by Friday, with all that grumbling laid out on the table in front of everyone, we look at a co-worker who's lost and say, "How would you like to come to church with me this Sunday?" You think your mouth doesn't affect people? That person isn't going to want to go anywhere near church with you!

> It's important for you to realize how powerful and influential your words are.

Acts chapter 2 shows us that what was happening that day was "noised abroad" and three thousand people came to the Lord. Why? Because somebody chose to testify rather than complain. Peter stepped up and said, "This is that which was spoken by the prophet Joel, that in the last days I will pour out of my Spirit upon all flesh…." You need to learn that when you open your mouth, it is going to directly affect other people. What are you saying in front of your children? They don't need to be hearing grumbling and complaining come out of your mouth. They need to hear you talking about "If God be for me, who can be against me." (Romans 8:31) They need to hear your mouth saying how you can do all things through Christ Jesus who strengthens you (Philippians 4:13). You need to learn how to speak and be careful because it affects your children.

James 1:26 says, *"If any man among you seem to be religious, and bridleth not his tongue, but deceiveth his own heart, this man's religion*

• • •

is vain." The key word here is *bridle*. You know what a bridle is. A bridle changes the direction. I ride horses at my dad's house. He's got a bridle and bit on that horse. Whenever I want to go to the right, I just pull on that rein and it turns the horse's head to the right. What the Word of God here is saying is that when you train your mouth, you train it to go the direction in which you really want to go. *You can direct your mouth with faith or you can direct your mouth with doubt.* You must make the choice to direct your mouth with faith, and we know that we please God that way.

> **Wherever your mouth directs or leads, your life will follow.**

Wherever your mouth directs or leads, your life will follow. This is how it works. "Well, I don't have any friends. Look where I'm headed. All my friends are over there. I don't have anybody here to be friends with. Nobody understands me. Nobody cares about me. There's nobody who really loves me." Before you know it, you're sitting there all alone, not because everybody feels that way about you. No, it's because your mouth led you over there all by yourself. It's not a matter of sitting in your house and crying, "Oh Lord, if You'd just send a friend to me." No. Be a friend. Learn how to direct your mouth. Train it as to where you want it to go.

Your mouth can bring about deliverance. Proverbs 12:6 tells us that, *"The words of the wicked are to lie in wait for blood: but the mouth of the upright shall deliver them."* Your mouth has the power to deliver.

> *And when they began to sing and to praise, the Lord set ambushments against the children of Ammon, Moab, and mount Seir, which were come against Judah; and they were smitten.* (2 Chronicles 20:22)

• • •

Notice when they began to sing and give praise, God sent ambushments against their enemies. You've got deliverance in your mouth. The Bible says they got all the spoil of their enemy. They didn't get it all because they had such a big sword or because they knew how to fight well. It happened because they knew how to give God praise in their given situation. They lifted up a praise. Early in the morning, the Bible says, they arose and they began to say, "Blessed is the Lord our God who is able to deliver us. Blessed is the Lord God." That's how you need to greet your new day when you wake up in the morning! "Blessed is the Lord my God who is able to do exceedingly, abundantly above all I could ever ask or think!" (Ephesians 3:20)

Your mouth feeds your life. Proverbs 12:18 declares, *"There is that speaketh like the piercings of a sword: but the tongue of the wise is health."* Again in Proverbs 16:24 we read, *"Pleasant words are as an honeycomb, sweet to the soul, and health to the bones."* Health. Pleasant words are like health to the bones. Some folks just keep living the same old lifestyle and talking the same old stuff. They scoff and say, "I've walked this path for twenty years. I'm still broke, still defeated. I've tried it all." That may be so, but you sure haven't tried training that mouth!

Proverbs 18:21, *"Death and life are in the power of the tongue: and they that love it shall eat the fruit thereof."* In other words, whatever I'm saying is what I'm going to have to grab up and eat. But now, go up one verse and read verse 20. *"A man's belly shall be satisfied with the fruit of his mouth; and with the increase of his lips shall he be filled."* It's not flipping through the TV channels chasing one great minister after another that's going to fill you. No, you need to understand that to be filled comes from the inside of you. They can encourage you, but they cannot fill you. But when you open your mouth and

• • •

speak, that's where your filling comes from! The increase of your lips will bring fulfillment to your life.

Start talking to yourself! Ephesians 5:19, *"Speaking to yourselves in psalms and hymns and spiritual songs, singing and making melody in your heart to the Lord."* You may be thinking, *now why exactly do I want to sing to myself?* The answer is in Romans 10:17: *"So then faith cometh by hearing, and hearing by the word of God."*

Spiritual songs are songs that don't necessarily rhyme. Sing to yourself because song brings melody. Melody brings a spirit of release and a feeling of excitement and happiness. Before you know it you've got joy. Start singing, "I am blessed." You start singing "Money cometh." Those are spiritual songs.

We are talking about giving yourself a mouth alert! Wake up your mouth to do what the Bible says to do. The reason this thing isn't really working for you is because you're not doing what the Word's telling you to do. Learn how to encourage yourself in the Lord.

Your mouth is a weapon. And it can paralyze the devil. Psalm 8:2, *"Out of the mouth of babes and sucklings hast thou ordained strength because of thine enemies, that thou mightest still the enemy and the avenger."* The word *still* in this verse means *to paralyze.* So when the devil's coming at you and you praise God, that paralyzes the devil. The minute you open your mouth with praise, the devil loses his nerve to take one more step in your direction.

What happens with too many Christians is that when they see the devil coming, they start trying to do things to stay away from him. But what I like about praise is that you don't even have to see the devil coming. The minute you lift up your praise, he's paralyzed right in his tracks. How do you keep him paralyzed constantly?

• • •

I will bless the Lord at all times: his praise shall continually be in my mouth! (Psalm 34:1)

Your mouth produces increase or decrease. Read what David has to say about the mouth and increase in Psalm 45:1-2.

My heart is inditing a good matter: I speak of the things which I have made touching the king: my tongue is the pen of a ready writer. Thou art fairer than the children of men: grace is poured into thy lips: therefore God hath blessed thee for ever.

But then in Deuteronomy 1:34-35 we read about the mouth and decrease.

And the LORD heard the voice of your words, and was wroth, and sware, saying, Surely there shall not one of these men of this evil generation see that good land, which I sware to give unto your fathers.

Notice that in both of these references, blessing and cursing, increase and decrease, were attached to their mouths. The reason people are increased or decreased is because of their mouths.

Use your mouth to speak the truth with wisdom. The King James Version of Proverbs 25:15 says, *"By long forbearing is a prince persuaded, and a soft tongue breaketh the bone."* The Living Bible states it like this, *"Be patient and you will finally win, for a soft tongue can break hard bones."* If your husband has a hard head, learn to speak softly to him and those soft words will break hard bones. Just as sure as your tongue can cause good, it can cause trouble. You know that's true! Psalm 39:1 says to *"keep my mouth with a bridle while the wicked is before me."* Oh my, we need to be careful what we say while the wicked are before us.

• • •

Truth should be held in tension. Imagine, if you will, that I have a water hose here in my hand. There's no nozzle on the end; it's just an open hose. Now imagine that the water is turned on and begins to flow through the hose. What's the water doing when it reaches the end of the hose? It's just bubbling out in a big soft flow, not going very far. But now see me hold my thumb over the opening of that hose so that the space for the water to come through is much smaller. You know what happens to the water then. It sprays way out from the hose. It affects a much larger area than it did with no tension on it.

The same is true with my words. If I just speak everything out, it's like that hose with the water just bubbling out. It doesn't affect a very big area at all. But when I hold my truth in tension, I can reach farther than I could the other way. When you release your truth little by little, it affects more lives than if you just let it all out at once.

You're sitting in your living room and you've got three lost family members there and you want to tell them everything they ought to know. So you start in on them with, "You should do this and you ought to do that," instead of just holding it and releasing small bits of truth to them. "God loves you just the way you are." That's more effective than telling them they have to change and rearrange. They'll get to that. But truth needs to be held in tension.

Never push the "pause" on your praise.

> *Let them shout for joy, and be glad, that favour my righteous cause: yea, let them say continually, Let the LORD be magnified, which hath pleasure in the prosperity of his servant. And my tongue shall speak of thy righteousness and of thy praise all the day long.* (Psalm 35:27-28)

• • •

Join with David, "I will bless the LORD at all times: his praise shall continually be in my mouth."

In the end, it will all add up.

For by thy words thou shalt be justified, and by thy words thou shalt be condemned. (Matthew 12:37)

It's not about your actions. God can forgive actions, but He can't stand a dirty mouth. By your words, it will all add up in the end. You're going to have to give an account for the way you talk. It's not just about how you talk about yourself. How are you talking about the anointing of God, the church and people in authority and leadership? Remember that you're going to eat whatever it is you condemn. You need to understand that your mouth determines your miracle. Put your mouth on alert and watch how much your life changes for the better!

• • •

. . .

Chapter 8

Canceled by Complaint

You know people who are hard to be around. They're so down in the mouth. The only words that come out of their mouths are complaints. This is wrong and that is wrong. Their testimony is that nothing ever works out right for them. You just know that when these folks go to heaven, they're going to walk in and their loved ones are going to run up to them and say, "Aren't you glad you're here!" And their response will be, "Humph! Had to die to get here. I guess it's beautiful enough, but I had to die to get here!" On their headstone will surely be carved "I expected this." I'm talking really negative folks!

> *And they took of the fruit of the land in their hands, and brought it down unto us, and brought us word again, and said, It is a good land which the LORD our God doth give us. Notwithstanding ye would not go up, but rebelled against the commandment of the LORD your God: And ye murmured in your tents, and said, Because the LORD hated us, he hath*

• • •

brought us forth out of the land of Egypt, to deliver us into the hand of the Amorites, to destroy us. Whither shall we go up? our brethren have discouraged our heart, saying, The people is greater and taller than we; the cities are great and walled up to heaven; and moreover we have seen the sons of the Anakims there. Then I said unto you, Dread not, neither be afraid of them. The LORD your God which goeth before you, he shall fight for you, according to all that he did for you in Egypt before your eyes; And in the wilderness, where thou hast seen how that the LORD thy God bare thee, as a man doth bear his son, in all the way that ye went, until ye came into this place. Yet in this thing ye did not believe the LORD your God, Who went in the way before you, to search you out a place to pitch your tents in, in fire by night, to shew you by what way ye should go, and in a cloud by day. And the LORD heard the voice of your words, and was wroth, and sware, saying, Surely there shall not one of these men of this evil generation see that good land, which I sware to give unto your fathers.... (Deuteronomy 1:25-35)

Notice verse 34 says that the Lord heard the voice of their words. Make that personal. *The Lord heard the voice of my words.* There are many people who have a complex of despair and agony about their past. Some things in our past just seem to put us through hell because we can't let go of what happened back there. And they never seem to be able to look out beyond the present to see the future. They're always holding onto a hurt or a disappointment. They make statements like this, "If something bad is going to happen, it's going to happen to me." They just live life with an expectation of something going wrong with their next step. We must understand that our mouth can either create a mountain or move one.

• • •

God is a God who is the same yesterday, today, and forever. He will not change. But God will not give that which you cancel. He won't go past your will to bless you. He will not cross your will; you must be obedient to His Word. Notice that we are not talking about things being delayed, but actually *canceled*. There are some things in your life that have not been delayed; they've been absolutely canceled. In this Scripture, their promise was not delayed. Their promise was not put off for a better day. It was absolutely, one hundred percent, unequivocally canceled because of their complaints.

You need to understand what God said to these folks earlier. Deuteronomy 1:6-8 gives us more insight into the situation.

> *The LORD our God spake unto us in Horeb, saying, Ye have dwelt long enough in this mount: Turn you, and take your journey, and go to the mount of the Amorites, and unto all the places nigh thereunto, in the plain, in the hills, and in the vale, and in the south, and by the sea side, to the land of the Canaanites, and unto Lebanon, unto the great river, the river Euphrates. Behold, I have set the land before you: go in and possess the land which the LORD sware unto your fathers, Abraham, Isaac, and Jacob, to give unto them and to their seed after them.*

God was saying, "It is time for you. You have been here long enough. It's time for you to arise and get out of Horeb." In the original Hebrew, the word *Horeb* means *Korab, to parch, to desolate, destroy, decay, to destroy by drying out, to slay or to make waste."* God was telling them that they'd been in a broken situation, a disgusted situation. They had been in a desolate and dry situation long enough. It was time to pack up and get out!

There situation didn't come about because of what they saw. Their problem occurred because of what somebody else saw. Their brethren had gone up to them and told them that it was really bad

• • •

over there (v. 28). If you want to maintain your promise with God, you need to get the losers out of your ear! You have to be able to quit worrying about what everybody else sees and says and start thinking about what God says! If you will latch onto what God says, you won't worry at all about what anybody else brings to you. Your attitude needs to become, "If God said it's my land, bless God, I don't care if giants are everywhere. This land is mine!"

> ...nobody can steal what God's promised you until you start talking like you've lost it.

We're talking about "canceled by complaint." Somebody thinks *Well, I messed up.* But nobody can steal what God's promised you until you start talking like you've lost it. Until God says it's over, it's just not over. *Well, I've committed adultery.* It's still not over. *But I lost my job.* It's not over. *I'm a drug addict.* It's not over. *I'm an alcoholic.* It's not over. *Well, I'm just not worth anything.* That's a lie! God says you've got a promise! Hold on to that promise!

The worst thing to me is when something gets canceled that you didn't even know was going to happen. It's bad enough to know this will never happen. But it's a whole other thing to never know what you could have had and never will. Lots of folks come right to the edge of their miracle, only to have it canceled by complaint. They keep on walking, but they lose the benefit that was waiting to overtake them.

It's so easy to go through life, not realizing what we're doing. When a bit of struggle comes your way, the words out of your mouth are, "Dear Lord, I'm dry! I can't believe it. I tithe. I give. But I'm dry. Lord, where are you? You know I can't break out of this poverty. I thought You were going to do something. I thought You

• • •

were going to show up for me. I thought You were going to bring a refreshing. It's always happening to me. If anybody's going to miss their blessing, it's going to be me." Through your complaining, you have just walked away from God and your blessing. He can't get it to you at that point. It's canceled.

In the sixth chapter of II Samuel, we find David dancing into Jerusalem. Taking off his kingly robes, he threw them on the ground and came into the city dancing. His wife, Michal, was looking out over the ledge and saw him. She immediately disapproved of what she saw. When David walked in, she unloaded on him big time. She started telling him exactly what she thought and how she felt about what he had done and about how terrible she thought he was for doing it. And we see a simple sentence at the end of her complaint:

Therefore Michal the daughter of Saul had no child unto the day of her death. (1 Samuel 6:23)

This story tells me a couple of things. First, there are times when you will cancel your blessing and never know that you are the reason for the cancellation. Second, God will not tolerate a complaining, murmuring, griping spirit. He cuts it off. I can hear God saying, "If the momma will do it, then the children will do it; I'm going to cut that thing off before it ever starts." He silenced her future because she couldn't control her mouth in her present. Her children represented what was to come in her life.

There was a lady in our church one day. Every time she saw me, she was complaining about pain in her body. Now, I was a young pastor, so I felt like I needed to pray for her every time I saw her. One day I was literally hiding from the woman. I'd come through closets to get to the church so she wouldn't find me. I'd open the door and she'd be there waiting on me, crying. I prayed, "Thank

• • •

You, Lord, for healing this sister from the top of her head to the souls of her feet. We command by the stripes of Jesus to be healed in Jesus' name. Praise the Lord." The next time we were in church, it was the same thing all over again. Time after time this happened.

It was just in her to complain. If you'd ask her how she was today, she'd respond, "Well, my ankle sure hurts."

The next day, "How are you doing?"

"Migraine."

"Well, how are you today?"

"Back hurts."

"How are you today, sister?"

"Oh, my neck hurts so bad."

Finally, after praying everything I knew to pray and after praying every way I knew to pray, I decided that I was just going to get this woman the next time I saw her. Sure enough, in the next service, here she came for prayer. So I just laid my hands on her and said, "Lord, today heal her or kill her in Jesus' name! Right now!" Man, she came out of that! I'd walk into the church after that and ask her, "How do you feel today?" And she would get all happy and say, "I'm healed! Whew!" It's amazing what you will do when you know this is it.

Think back to Michal. If it was never planned for Michal to conceive, then God would have never canceled her conception. If she was never going to have had kids, then God would not have canceled the kids. Because of what He was going to do, He took it away from her because of her complaint.

I remembered God, and was troubled: I complained, and my spirit was overwhelmed. Selah. (Psalm 77:3)

• • •

I don't have a Ph.D., but I can tell you this. If you want to break out of depression, quit complaining. That's number one. Quit looking at the circumstances and start looking at the answers. If there's a problem, there is an answer. If there's something you can't solve, there is a solution somewhere. God will make a way for you because God does not promise what He cannot deliver. It has nothing to do with us except for our praise and our willingness to possess what He has promised us. Unfortunately, there are some people who are going to lose some things because they have perfected complaining.

But there are those others who understand that to complain is to lose, but that to give God praise causes you to possess all that God has promised for your life! God has some things in store for you if you will learn how to give Him praise through the bad times and the good times, through the rain as well as the sunshine, through the trial and the tribulation, through the circumstance and through the sorrow as well as in times of joy. When you learn to walk in that praise and give

> When you learn to walk in that praise and give God the glory, then you will experience God making a way for you where there seems to be no way.

God the glory, then you will experience God making a way for you where there seems to be no way. When the mountain is too high, and the valley is too low, and the river is too deep, God will part the waters for you to walk through on dry ground! As long as you've got a praise, you've got a future. As long as you've got a praise, you've got a promise from God.

The second time I ever preached in my life was in a church of about twelve hundred black folks. I had never experienced church like

• • •

that before! I was hollering and they were hollering right back to me. It was awesome and we were having so much fun! However, within ten minutes of my starting, I had said everything I had planned on saying in a full hour! I mean, I had closed; I was finished! Just about that time, you're searching around for something more to say, something more to do. "Lord, Lord, what do I do now?"

It was obvious to me that God really did want to do something in the service, but what. Then I heard Him say to me, "Give away your watch." Now my watch was a brand new Rolex that I had just bought. It was my prized possession, my pride and joy. So, my immediate response to the Lord was, "I bind you, Satan, in the name of Jesus!" He said it to my heart again, "Give away your watch." There I was struggling with His words when I heard Him say, "You must be satisfied with what you have and not ready for what I have for you. Forget it."

Well, that got my attention! "Okay, Lord, I'll do it. Who do You want me to give it to?" God told me to turn around and when I did, there was an old black brother sitting on the stage sleeping. I thought *Surely, Lord, I've had a thousand people jumping and screaming 'preach it!' You aren't going to make me give my Rolex to somebody's who's been sleeping on me, are you?'* Still I heard, "Give it to him."

So, I walked over there and woke him up. He woke with a start and an "Amen! That's right! Glory! Do what the Lord says! Say it!" I reached out to him and told him that the Lord had instructed me to give him my Rolex. He jumped up and grabbed that watch and just took off running around the building. People starting jumping and shouting and dancing. That was it. Folks went crazy. The service was over.

After leaving church later, I found myself in Underground Atlanta to have some lunch. After eating I walked into a clothing store to buy

• • •

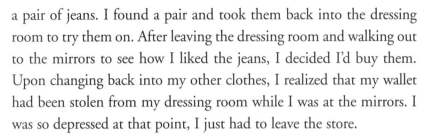

a pair of jeans. I found a pair and took them back into the dressing room to try them on. After leaving the dressing room and walking out to the mirrors to see how I liked the jeans, I decided I'd buy them. Upon changing back into my other clothes, I realized that my wallet had been stolen from my dressing room while I was at the mirrors. I was so depressed at that point, I just had to leave the store.

The walk back to my van was a pretty silent one. I was not happy. As we approached the van, I realized it didn't look right. Sure enough, all the windows had been broken out of it. Besides all the glass being in pieces, the culprits had climbed in and stolen my VCR and everything else I had in there. I drove to the convenience store across the street and bought a box of Glad bags to cover the gaping holes where the windows used to be. I was wondering, *What do I have to be glad about? Don't have my Rolex. Don't have any money. And my van has just been busted up.* Driving down the highway with plastic bags covering all the window holes…van windows are huge…it made noise like an army was shooting at you. About that time somebody said, "I'm hungry. What time is it?" I thought, *How should I know? I don't have a watch; I can't tell time.'*

Have you ever been there before and know what I'm talking about? It's bad! Right before I opened my mouth to complain, my little four-year-old daughter started singing in her car seat: I've got a feelin' everything's gonna be all right." Before long we were all laughing and crying and singing. People were driving past and wondering what in the world happened with that bunch!

Two days later I got a call from the father of one of my friends. He was in town and asked me to go to lunch with him. So I did. He asked if we could go in my car, but I told him that wouldn't be possible. So he pulled up to get me in a rented Mercedes. On the way to the restaurant, he asked if I minded stopping to look at something.

• • •

He pulled into a Mercedes dealership. We get out and start looking around at all the cars. He said, "Clint, if you were picking a car, which one would you pick?"

I thought, *If you only knew! We don't have anything!* I said, "Well, I don't…"

He said, "Do you like this one? Isn't this nice?"

I said, "Yeah." Well, then he wanted to take it for a test drive. So we drove all around. When we got back the salesman asked, "So, how do you want to finance that?"

The man said, "I don't want to finance it. We're going to pay cash."

And right in that moment, I wanted to get angry. *This guy's got all the cash! I'm sitting here broke!* But do you know what I said instead? I said, "My day's coming. I know it's coming." I stayed outside while they went inside and did all the paperwork. After a while, my friend's dad came back out with the keys in his hand. He walked up to me and tossed the keys to me. With that he said, "I hope you enjoy your new Mercedes!"

Another two days passed. I received a call from a gentleman I had ministered to previously. He was in town and wanted to know if I wanted to go to lunch.

"Sure, I'll go to lunch." So I pull up in my Mercedes to get him and we went to lunch. He asked me if I minded stopping by the mall on the way; he needed to go to the jewelry store. We walked into the store and he headed straight for a case of Rolex watches. He said, "Clint, if you were going to pick…."

This man bought a Rolex for me that was worth more than twice the one I had given away. Psalm 65:1 tells us that *Praise waiteth for thee, O God…* I had never noticed this before. It doesn't mean

• • •

that *I am going to withhold until.* It means *meet me at the church! I will be waiting on you!"*

When I saw this in the Scriptures, I heard God speak to my heart, "When you began to praise me that day in your van instead of complaining about your losses and your circumstances, your praise had already gone before the Mercedes. Your praise had already gone before the Rolex watch."

After going to the jewelry store and then to lunch, I drove the man back to his lodging. Before he left me he said, "Clint, come here. Hold out your hand. He started counting out hundred dollar bills into my hand. Twenty of them, to be exact. Why? The devil stole $200 from me in Atlanta. But God gave me $2000 back just weeks later because I gave God my praise! We possess it with our praise.

Before we ever get to the battle, our praise must already have been there. Before we ever get to the circumstance, our praise must already have been there. We must be able to say with David, "My praise is waiting for you, God!"

• • •

• • •

Chapter 9

This Praise Is for You

———◆———

I'll never forget the time my parents visited. I thought I'd be nice and treat them to a suite in the best hotel in Orlando. I was excited to tell them, "You two are getting the Presidential Suite. It is an awesome place! It's going to blow your mind. You're going to love it!" When they arrived I had a limo meet them and take them to their hotel.

After a couple of days they left the hotel and came to my home. I was sitting where they didn't know I could here them talking, and I heard my mom saying, "You better not say a word! Don't you say one word!" So I walked into the room where they were and my dad said, "I have to say it!"

Dad went on, "Son, you said that suite over there was a presidential suite. I have to be honest with you; how much does that room cost?"

"It's $1500 a night," I replied.

"Well, somebody's robbing you!"

• • •

"What are you talking about, Dad," I asked.

Mom tried to stop him from speaking further, but he turned to her and said, "Listen, I have to tell the boy in case he puts somebody else up there and they think they're getting something special." Then turning back to me he began to explain. "We got to our room and we were shocked. There wasn't a bathtub; I had to shower in there. I had to pull our bed out of the wall."

"What!"

"Oh yeah," he said.

I was consternated. "Were you on the fifteenth floor?" I asked.

"Yes, we were."

I said, "Did you have to put your key into the little slot there in the elevator and press your button to get up there?"

"Yes, we did."

"Were you on the concierge level where you could go eat at five and eat breakfast in the morning?"

"Yeah, yeah," dad said, mom agreeing with a nod of her head.

"No, no," I said, "Something's wrong here."

He said, "I'm telling you the truth now."

I said, "Well, we're going to be having dinner there tonight. I want you to show me what you're talking about." So we arrived at the hotel that night and I found the manager, whom I knew well. We got into the elevator and went to the fifteenth floor. When we entered the room, I said, "This is nice. Now let's look at the bedroom."

Dad said, "What do you mean?"

I said, "Dad, this is just the lounging area right here. This is your living room."

• • •

Now it was dad's turn to be confused. "What are you talking about?" he asked.

"Dad, how many keys did they give you when you checked in?" I asked with a smile.

"Oh, they gave me two or three packs of keys, but I only needed one of them," he replied.

"Dad, this key opens this door and this other key opens this door and that key there opens that other door. You have 2200 square feet of rooms and you and mom slept and stayed in 240 feet of it!"

"Just leave me on the farm next time!" he quipped back at me. Dad hadn't realized that he had a key and that he had access. It was his, but he didn't know anything about it. How many of you know that if you just understood even half of what God has already put on the inside you, that the enemy would be no match to what you have. You

Praise can change the atmosphere of what the enemy is trying to do in your life.

just have to realize you have it…and let it come out!

You might be walking through the greatest storm of your life. Praise can change the atmosphere of what the enemy is trying to do in your life. If you can understand that you have to lift up your voice in the midst of your situation and release unto God what He deserves and what He inhabits, your situation will change. The enemy's plan against your life will be altered.

Paul and Silas found themselves in a serious situation, recorded in the sixteenth chapter of Acts. When the people who were uncomfortable with the move of God that Paul and Silas brought to the

• • •

city, they went before the magistrates saying, "You must put them in prison and you must beat them in public before you do it, so the people of the city can know that they cannot support such worship here." So they took Paul and Silas and beat them and put them in prison. Oh, they didn't put them just anywhere. No, the Bible says that they were in the inner part of the prison.

I have been to Israel three times. On one of the trips we stopped back in Rome and did television in some of the synagogues and coliseums there. I was able to visit some of the prisons and places that are mentioned in Scripture. The inner chamber of a prison was that place where they put people and chained them to the wall. People on the outside would bring the human waste from their homes each day because they had no sewage systems, and they would pour it down into the center of the prison to add aggravatin to all of the prisoners in that inner chamber.

Paul and Silas did nothing wrong, yet they found themselves beaten half to death, chained to the walls in the inner chamber of the prison.

> And the multitude rose up together against them: and the magistrates rent off their clothes, and commanded to beat them. And when they had laid many stripes upon them, they cast them into prison, charging the jailor to keep them safely: Who, having received such a charge, thrust them into the inner prison, and made their feet fast in the stocks. (Acts 16:22-24)

They had this raw sewage dumped on top of them all day. They had people spit on them and talk about them. The wounds on their backs were open and bleeding, infected from all the filth they were forced to stay in.

• • •

That's pretty bleak, isn't it. Do you think they could have felt discouraged, disheartened, and depressed? Maybe it was a good time for them to give up and say, "I'm done with all this stuff." It was midnight, the darkest part of the night, the darkest place in their circumstances. Verse 25 tells us exactly what they did: *"And at midnight Paul and Silas prayed, and sang praises unto God: and the prisoners heard them."* Paul and Silas decided that the circumstance around them was no match for what was on the inside of them.

Notice that the prisoners chained to the walls in the prison heard Paul and Silas as they praised. When you're going through a tough issue in your life, what do people hear coming out of your mouth on Monday morning when you get to the job? What are they hearing on the other side of the cubicle while you're typing on your computer or talking on your cell phone on a break? When you're in the lunchroom talking to someone about what you're going through, what are they hearing come out of you? Some of those around you may be going through a hellish situation of their own. One word from you can alter their situation. It's important what you say. Sometimes you're going to give praise to get yourself through your situation, but there are other times when you're going to give God praise for the benefit of others besides yourself.

The Word says that the prisoners heard Paul and Silas giving praise to God. They heard something coming from the inner part of the prison. They must have thought, *What are those two doing? They smell bad and their backs are bleeding and infected, but they're in there singing praises to God.* Somehow Paul and Silas had mustered enough strength on the inside of them to begin to give God praise.

Look at what happened in response to their praise.

And suddenly there was a great earthquake, so that the foundations of the prison were shaken: and immediately all the doors

were opened, and every one's bands were loosed. And the keeper of the prison awaking out of his sleep, and seeing the prison doors open, he drew out his sword, and would have killed himself, supposing that the prisoners had been fled. But Paul cried with a loud voice, saying, Do thyself no harm: for we are all here. (Acts 16:26-28)

Wow! Think about it. Two men lying in a prison cell start praising God in the middle of the night. All of a sudden, an earthquake hits, all the doors fly open, and the chains fall off of ALL the prisoners in the place! What a miracle! And then, on top of all that, the jailer runs in, sees the doors open, figures all the prisoners have run off, so he pulls out his sword to kill himself before his superiors could do it for him. The voice of Paul speaks out from the chaos that moment must have felt like: "Don't kill yourself; we're all here." That's another miracle! Nobody ran off!

Don't you think you might have been tempted to dash out of the prison and save yourself immediately? After all, look what had happened. God had obviously shown up on the scene and made a way out for them. Yet, here is Paul saying, "We're all here. Don't worry." You see, Paul and Silas didn't praise God in order to get out. What happened next?

Then he called for a light, and sprang in, and came trembling, and fell down before Paul and Silas, And brought them out, and said, Sirs, what must I do to be saved? And they said, Believe on the Lord Jesus Christ, and thou shalt be saved, and thy house. And they spake unto him the word of the Lord, and to all that were in his house. And he took them the same hour of the night, and washed their stripes; and was baptized, he and all his, straightway. And when he had brought them into his

• • •

house, he set meat before them, and rejoiced, believing in God with all his house. (Acts 16:29-34)

A sermon couldn't do it. A testimony couldn't do it. But somebody's praise was powerful enough to bring a Roman soldier, who had never heard the gospel, to a place of accepting Jesus into his heart. And not just the Roman soldier, but his whole family, too! It is vital that you realize that your praise is not just for your own benefit. Your praise can reach the soul of somebody else who doesn't know anything about Jesus. Because they watch you praise in the midst of your situation, they decide, "I want what you've got!" You thought your praise was just to get you out of your own circumstances. But when you see how the other person is touched, you can say to them, "This praise was for you!" The jailer asked, "What must I do to be saved?" His heart must have been thinking, *Give me what it takes to sing in the middle of the night. Tell me what you have that causes you to bless the Lord when you're down in your body. Tell me what you took that causes you to sing a song when everything's going wrong in your life."*

> It is vital that you realize that your praise is not just for your own benefit.

The jailer took Paul and Silas to his house. There he fed them and washed their wounds and put medicine on them. He fed them and took care of them…and he and his household were saved and baptized that same night! This all started at midnight! I imagine that at some point the jailer said he had best be getting back to the jail. And Paul would have said, "Wait up, we're going with you."

And the keeper of the prison told this saying to Paul, The magistrates have sent to let you go: now therefore depart, and go in peace. But Paul said unto them, They have beaten us openly uncondemned, being Romans, and have cast us into prison; and

• • •

now do they thrust us out privily? nay verily; but let them come themselves and fetch us out. And the serjeants told these words unto the magistrates: and they feared, when they heard that they were Romans. And they came and besought them, and brought them out, and desired them to depart out of the city. And they went out of the prison, and entered into the house of Lydia and when they had seen the brethren, they comforted them, and departed. (Acts 16:36-40)

How the jailer may have scratched his head and wondered about these two! *Why would you go back there?* must have been running through his head. Paul was saying to the magistrates, "You made fun of us in public. You beat us in public. You laughed at us in public. Don't set us free in private now. If you're going to bless me, bless me where folks who've been laughing at me can watch you bless me.

I'll never forget the time I was invited to preach to thousands and thousands of people. I gave it my all. When I finished, I was exhausted, tired, wrung out. I just grabbed my Bible and my stuff and started to walk off the stage. The pastor, though, grabbed the microphone and said, "Hold it! If you think you're going to leave here without singing at least one song, you're crazy!" I said to myself, *Man, you're the one who's crazy! I'm about to pass out up here I'm so tired. My vocal chords are lying somewhere in my Bible, wherever I was preaching.* I didn't hardly have any voice left as I walked back up to the pulpit. Finally, after continuing to argue internally for another few moments, I just picked up a mic, turned to the brother sitting at the piano and told him to play something. And a song began to pour forth from within me.

Later, in the pastor's study, a man who had been standing in the very back of the room during the whole service pulled me aside and said, "I decided tonight that I was going to blow my brains out

• • •

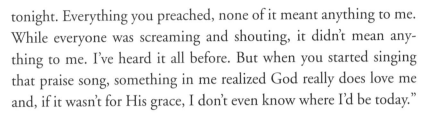

tonight. Everything you preached, none of it meant anything to me. While everyone was screaming and shouting, it didn't mean anything to me. I've heard it all before. But when you started singing that praise song, something in me realized God really does love me and, if it wasn't for His grace, I don't even know where I'd be today."

That pastor tapped me on the shoulder to tell me, "See, you did not feel like singing, but you weren't singing for yourself!" Every time I praise Him, it's not always about me. Sometimes this praise is for you.

The people you face on a daily basis have so much hell in their lives, so many troubles and trials. Do you know what they're listening for? Is there a ray of hope? No wonder God didn't attach faith to our eyes. Eyes can tell a circumstance is hopeless, but He said faith cometh by hearing. I like the fact that they put Paul and Silas in prison and that it was midnight because they couldn't see everybody else's situation. No, it was dark and their praise was the light that said, "We're all on an even playing field. We're all going through something. Your praise can have a powerful impact on someone around you!

• • •

...

Chapter 10

The Price of Praise

I grew up in an extraordinary traditional church that made me ask questions about God and His way of doing things. Let me tell you that in my church, it was considered a sin for a woman to wear pantyhose. That was because the legs were connected, you see, and you therefore had to put them on one leg at a time, and that meant you were wearing pants, which was men's apparel. Oh yeah. They were for real!

So I grew up with a spirit of questioning the God I was encouraged to serve. *Why can't I do this? Why can't I do that?* Anytime you are raised in such a legalistic environment, it seems like all the "can'ts" and "don'ts" are so big that you lose sight of the "cans" and "dos". Walking up to the pastor and asking him a question about what he had just preached was a huge no-no!

It seemed like people never really wanted me to ask questions. I understand why they were aggravated with me because sometimes

• • •

your kids just aren't satisfied with your answers. When your kids were little, did you ever say, "You can't do that." What was the first thing out of the child's mouth: Why? Don't we all know the famous answer back: Because. Or we'll put a little extra on it with "Because I said so!" None of that made any sense at all to the child who wants a valid explanation of why they can't.

The book of Job presents situations that made me wonder about God. In the first chapter, first verse we find a good man: *There was a man in the land of Uz, whose name was Job; and that man was perfect and upright, and one that feared God, and eschewed evil.* To eschew evil means that he ran away from evil. He walked away from bad things. Job was a good man!

God chose this man to do something that made me want to question. Follow along as the story begins to unfold:

And there was a day when his sons and his daughters were eating and drinking wine in their eldest brother's house: And there came a messenger unto Job, and said, The oxen were plowing, and the asses feeding beside them: And the Sabeans fell upon them, and took them away; yea, they have slain the servants with the edge of the sword; and I only am escaped alone to tell thee. While he was yet speaking, there came also another, and said, The fire of God is fallen from heaven, and hath burned up the sheep, and the servants, and consumed them; and I only am escaped alone to tell thee. While he was yet speaking, there came also another, and said, The Chaldeans made out three bands, and fell upon the camels, and have carried them away, yea, and slain the servants with the edge of the sword; and I only am escaped alone to tell thee. While he was yet speaking, there came also another, and said, Thy sons and thy daughters were eating and drinking wine in their eldest brother's house: And, behold, there came a great wind from the

• • •

wilderness, and smote the four corners of the house, and it fell upon the young men, and they are dead; and I only am escaped alone to tell thee. Then Job arose, and rent his mantle, and shaved his head, and fell down upon the ground, and worshipped, And said, Naked came I out of my mother's womb, and naked shall I return thither: the LORD gave, and the LORD hath taken away; blessed be the name of the LORD. In all this Job sinned not, nor charged God foolishly. (Job 1:13-22)

I think most of us believers do not have a problem serving God when trouble comes our way. When trouble shows up, most of us do not have a problem going through it with an attitude of knowing that God is going to fix it. The reason for that is because when most of us were saved in that original time when we came to God, somebody told us that we were going to have everything ultimately turn out all right. We might have trouble come to us from time to time, but we would always know that everything was going to turn out all right. The biggest problem in that is the fact they couldn't tell us *when* it was all going to be all right.

Because of that, we have birthed Christians who got saved, but when trouble came the next day and God didn't have it all fixed by the day after that, they dropped out of church because of their disappointment in God. So, there's an internal conflict going on between what you believe and what you expect when it doesn't happen in the timing and in the way you wanted it to happen.

The circumstance here with Job is questionable because we find that this man is going through something huge. It's not because he's an evil man. It's not happening because he did something wrong. He didn't mess up or make a mistake. You can make some sense of your own situation in a time of trouble because you can many times look back and see the reason why you're walking through the problem.

• • •

But looking at Job here, why did God allow something to happen in this man's life? Job is declared perfect in the first verse of the book. That word *perfect* doesn't mean that he had no flaws. It means *the process of being perfected.* He was in the process of being perfected; he was upright and one who feared the Lord.

I can tell you right now, if somebody else is bragging on me, that's one thing. But when God himself declares something about me, it doesn't matter what anybody else says. Whatever God says is the way it really is. When God says, "You're all right," then I'm all right! I don't need a pat on the back from anybody else to let me know I'm doing well. As long as God says He will never leave me or forsake me, then it doesn't matter who forsakes me, leaves me, walks out, turns their back on me. I will stand the test of time knowing God is not going to leave me.

> ...when God himself declares something about me, it doesn't matter what anybody else says.

Yet, it can sometimes become discouraging when you are in a tough situation and you look back over your past, over yesterday, and you don't see anything that explains what you're going through today. You can't find anything back there that merits the pain you're experiencing. Slowly the realization comes that sometimes it's not the devil, but it's God. Mmmm! Sometimes it's God.

Job 2:3 shows us something:

And the LORD said unto Satan, Hast thou considered my servant Job, that there is none like him in the earth, a perfect and an upright man, one that feareth God, and escheweth evil? and still he holdeth fast his integrity, although thou movedst me against him, to destroy him without cause.

• • •

Sometimes God is going to allow certain situations to come into your life. God wants to do something in your life to bring Him glory.

You need to see the whole picture with Job. Satan came to God in a conversation. He started declaring to God that he had been roaming about the earth, seeking out whom he could find who would turn their back on God. And then Satan said something that made God angry. He said, "The only reason Job is serving You is because of what You're doing for him." God is going to let the devil see that we can go through a little bit of hell and still give the Lord a praise. We can go through some stuff and still have the sacrifice of praise. God is going to allow things to come into your life that will make you worship the Lord, even when you don't feel like it. When you feel like giving up, you're going to get up and lift your voice of praise. If there's one thing the devil just doesn't understand at all, it's somebody giving God praise even in that midnight hour. The devil thinks that when he fires his best shot at you, it ought to knock you out.

In essence, we need to understand that no relationship that is tied to dollars and cents is really a true relationship because I can pay anybody to love me. I can pay anybody to "amen" me. I can pay you to brag on me. I can pay you enough money to where you're afraid to say anything against me. I think God likes to see people who will love Him and who will praise Him even when everything's not going just right, when everything seems to be going wrong. God likes to see somebody who doesn't expect Him to write them a check in order to get a *thank you.*

As you read through the story of Job, you watch as he loses his sons and daughters. They represented his future. He loses his camels and oxen and sheep. They represented his fortune. Along with losing his fortune, he also lost his influence. You know people don't treat you the same when you run out of money. Everybody's your

• • •

friend when you have the cash. But when you lose the money, all of a sudden your phone stops ringing. Nobody's calling you.

The man lost his fortune. He lost his future. He lost his influence and his friends. Job's sitting down and thinking *Man, everything's gone. They killed my kids and my herds. There's nothing to go back to.* Job found himself thrust into a great unknown. Some of you would like to go back in your own life, but the door's been shut behind you. It's final. You can't get to the next place by always glancing back at what you had. Looking back freezes your future. Lot's wife was told, "Don't turn around." It wasn't because she couldn't look back, but because God wanted her to know that looking back means you are not going forward. You will always move in the direction of your focus. The door behind you is closed. Look ahead.

Job had a decision to make. His whole world had come crashing in on him. Everything looked down and out. All seemed lost. There was no one there beside him to pat him on the shoulder and say, "Hey, it's okay. You're going to make it." No, his friends came to tell him that he must have done something bad for all this to happen. Everyone had turned against him. How did it feel for friends to become foes? What was he going to do?

The thing he had feared the most had come upon him. He'd had it all and now he had nothing. Maybe it would have felt more possible to rebound if he could have had just a little bit to start rebuilding with. He had nothing. What could he do? Even his wife, the one he looked to for understanding and love, turned on him. In Job 2:9 she makes a crushing statement to him: *Then said his wife unto him, Dost thou still retain thine integrity? curse God, and die.* This was a sarcastic remark. The Living Bible puts it this way: *Are you still trying to be godly when God has done all this to you? Curse him and die.*

• • •

Look at his reply to her: *But he said unto her, Thou speakest as one of the foolish women speaketh. What? shall we receive good at the hand of God, and shall we not receive evil? In all this did not Job sin with his lips.* (verse 10) He was saying, "God has given me a lot of stuff. I may not understand it all, but He's decided to allow it to be taken away. But with or without the stuff, I'm still going to give Him praise. And until the next door opens, I will praise Him!"

God understands that, with an attitude like Job's in this, He was going to do something greater after the storm than what He had done before the storm ever arrived. Job had lost everything. The door was closed. So what was Job going to do?

> *Then Job arose, and rent his mantle, and shaved his head, and fell down upon the ground, and worshipped, And said, Naked came I out of my mother's womb, and naked shall I return thither: the LORD gave, and the LORD hath taken away; blessed be the name of the LORD.* (Job 1:20-21)

Allow me to paraphrase this for you. Job was saying this, "Naked I came into the world from my mother's womb and naked shall I return. The Lord gave and the Lord has taken away. I've got just one thing to say between the taking away and the giveth: Blessed, blessed, blessed be the name of the Lord!" The original meaning of that word *blessed* is *to give God praise*. Job was saying, "I got loose of everything I thought I'd always have. And the door of finality closed on me. But when I turned around, I still had my praise. I still had my thanksgiving. I still had my answer. I still had my admiration. I still had my glory to give back to the Lord.

Let me tell you why Job still had a praise. Out of everything God created in Genesis, the Bible says He did one thing with man that He didn't do with any other creation. He took His holy knee and rubbed it in the surface of the crusty earth and He breathed His

• • •

breath into man. And God said, "The only thing I expect back is what I give you. I gave you breath, and you ought to give me back a praise."

In the last chapter of the book of Job the end of the experience for Job was that God turned his captivity and restored back to him much much more than he had before. His fortunes were restored. His future was restored in that he knew his children into four generations! His influence was restored as were his relationships. *"So the LORD blessed the latter end of Job more than his beginning.... So Job died, being old and full of days."* (Job 42:12, 17)

You may be going through trials right here and now. You may be in one of life's storms today. You don't see any way out. Praise Him! You wonder if you're going to even make it. Give the Lord praise! Where your own door of finality has closed behind you, do what Job did. Arise from here and give God praise! Here in the middle where you don't know how your situation will work out, you just know that it will because God's God, right here, begin to praise Him! Bring Him glory with your praise!

• • •

Chapter 11

Can I Catch A Ride?

———◆———

Have you ever had to catch a ride with somebody? You may not really think so much about it at the time. Maybe your car broke down. Maybe you missed the bus or the plane and you end up making some other kind of travel arrangements. The proverbial hitchhiker that we see on virtually every road from time to time is the epitome of someone catching a ride. No matter what the circumstances were that created your predicament, the bottom line was the fact that you didn't have the ability to get yourself there on your own, so somebody picked you up and took you where you needed to be. That's the very thing we're talking about here.

God is truly a unique God. If God was like us, we'd sure be in trouble today, wouldn't we! One thing I love about God is that He sees everything. He can survey every aspect of everything. I also love the fact that, even when God knows what you're going to do, He doesn't disqualify you from where you are. We could stand to be more like that! When we know certain things about each other, we

• • •

tend to disqualify one another based on that information. God is very different from that.

Sometimes I don't understand how God can let me go through some certain circumstances and deal with some issues. But God is awesome in His ways. One day He told Abraham, *"Look now toward heaven, and tell the stars, if thou be able to number them: and he said unto him, So shall thy seed be."* (Genesis 15:5) God gave him a promise. To fulfill that promise, He announces to Abraham (His name was Abram before all this adventure began), "You're going to have a son." To understand the whole story, read the account in Genesis 16-21.

God is funny in some ways because He oftentimes lets us get down to the impossibility before He does anything. He'll lead five thousand folks out of town and let them get hungry just so He can take five loaves and two fishes and do a miracle. That's just the way He is. Now I just imagine that if God were to step in right now and give you what He wanted to give you, you might think it was your education that got you there. Some of you would think that it must have been that investment you made that put you where you are. If you have just a little bit of influence in your community, you might think it's who you know that got you where you are. So sometimes we come down to having nothing. He'll let you get to a place where, when you tell folks what God's said to you, they just laugh and say you're crazy. Oh, but God steps back and says, "Get ready!"

So Abraham was one man in the house with two women, his wife Sarai (Her name later became Sarah) and her maidservant Hagar. Sarai, at her age of ninety, couldn't have seemed very qualified to receive the promise of God. The natural mind had to wonder, *How can this be at her age?* In fact, Hebrews 11:11 tells us that she was past age. Hagar, on the other hand, must have seemed more qualified, younger, and more able in her own strength to bear a child.

• • •

The Bible says Abraham and Sarah waited a long time for the promise to come. The worst thing you can do is to try to get ahead of what God said He was going to do. Anything premature needs outside, artificial help to survive. But it must have just seemed like such a great idea, helping God figure out how He's going to do it. It's a bit like thinking you're going to show God His options! Yes, their plan seemed like a really good idea, logical, and doable. So they put it into motion. But, do you know that God really doesn't need our help!

In these two women we see a type and shadow. Sarah is a representation of the spirit; Hagar represents the flesh. Hagar produced a son named Ishmael, which represents the law of God. He had great blessing with an earthly promised land. He is as the sands of the sea. Isaac, on the other hand, came out of Sarah. She was the first bride of choice, but the second woman of relationship. She always represents the spirit because man understands his flesh more quickly than he understands his spirit. Sarah represents grace and promise. Man will attend to his flesh more quickly than he will learn to lean on his spirit.

Ishmael is the product of Hagar. Isaac is the product of Sarai. God spoke to Abraham and Abraham decided to get ahead of God. Abraham was drawn to his flesh and went in unto Hagar. He is just as incapable as Sarah, but he's convinced that what God hasn't done, he can do for God. So he has a son named Ishmael—the product of disobedience. Oh, but God is so awesome in His ways. He will allow you to impregnate outside of His will so you can get out of you what He wants out of you. Then you don't put Ishmael in Sarah and mess up His plan! Yes, God will get that stuff out of you! He will find a way.

We read in reference to Isaac, *"And the child grew, and was weaned: and Abraham made a great feast the same day that Isaac was weaned. And Sarah saw the son of Hagar the Egyptian, which she had born unto Abraham, mocking."* (Genesis 21:8-9) Hagar was a bondwoman, a

• • •

slave. She had no choice but to do what Abraham had said. Her will was not in place. In this passage we read that what Hagar's flesh produced was now mocking what the spirit (Sara) had produced.

That same thing takes place today. Comedians have made a mockery of the moving of the Holy Spirit. We always want to criticize what we don't understand. We must be mindful not to do that in our own lives. If you don't speak in tongues, don't criticize those who do. If you don't understand the Holy Spirit, don't be critical of His workings. God will hold your flesh accountable for what you do against the spirit.

In the next verse, listen to the words of Sarah about this matter:

Wherefore she said unto Abraham, Cast out this bondwoman and her son: for the son of this bondwoman shall not be heir with my son, even with Isaac. (Genesis 21:10)

There's a key right there. Notice that she did not say "instead of." She said "with." There are just some things that God cannot give to you until you learn to move outside of flesh and into the spirit. If you try to put them together, then you cannot inherit everything God has for you. You don't know how to put your flesh down. You can't operate by your flesh in a spirit kingdom. You're going to have to tell your flesh to pack its bags and go. It has to stop controlling your mind and your desires and everything else in your life.

Sarah was saying that flesh and spirit cannot coexist and inherit anything. Why? The reason is because a double-minded man should not think he can receive anything of God. (James 1:8) God's kind of funny. He lets trouble show up! The original Scripture says, *And Ishmael was adverse to Isaac.* This is a picture of your flesh fighting what your spirit is trying to do.

• • •

God always sets you up to qualify you by trouble, not triumph. From those hard places come our defining moments. God lets adversity come in order to be able to show you how to go and how to divide. It makes sense that types and shadows follow generations. Abraham was in a house with two women. Two children were birthed, representing flesh and spirit. One was a slave; one was free. One had to be there; the other one chose to be there. Abraham fathered a son named Isaac. Isaac grew into a man and had a son named Jacob.

God always sets you up to qualify you by trouble, not triumph.

Jacob ended up in a house with two women. The account is found in the twenty-ninth chapter of Genesis.

And it came to pass, when Jacob saw Rachel the daughter of Laban his mother's brother, and the sheep of Laban his mother's brother, that Jacob went near, and rolled the stone from the well's mouth, and watered the flock of Laban his mother's brother. And Jacob kissed Rachel, and lifted up his voice, and wept. And Jacob told Rachel that he was her father's brother, and that he was Rebekah's son: and she ran and told her father.

And it came to pass, when Laban heard the tidings of Jacob his sister's son, that he ran to meet him, and embraced him, and kissed him, and brought him to his house. And he told Laban all these things. And Laban said to him, Surely thou art my bone and my flesh. And he abode with him the space of a month. And Laban said unto Jacob, Because thou art my brother, shouldest thou therefore serve me for nought? tell me, what shall thy wages be? And Laban had two daughters: the name of the elder was Leah, and the name of the younger was Rachel. Leah was tender eyed; but Rachel was beautiful and well

• • •

favoured. And Jacob loved Rachel; and said, I will serve thee seven years for Rachel thy younger daughter. And Laban said, It is better that I give her to thee, than that I should give her to another man: abide with me. And Jacob served seven years for Rachel; and they seemed unto him but a few days, for the love he had to her. And Jacob said unto Laban, Give me my wife, for my days are fulfilled, that I may go in unto her. And Laban gathered together all the men of the place, and made a feast. And it came to pass in the evening, that he took Leah his daughter, and brought her to him; and he went in unto her. And Laban gave unto his daughter Leah Zilpah his maid for an handmaid. And it came to pass, that in the morning, behold, it was Leah: and he said to Laban, What is this thou hast done unto me? did not I serve with thee for Rachel? wherefore then hast thou beguiled me? And Laban said, It must not be so done in our country, to give the younger before the firstborn. Fulfil her week, and we will give thee this also for the service which thou shalt serve with me yet seven other years. And Jacob did so, and fulfilled her week: and he gave him Rachel his daughter to wife also. And Laban gave to Rachel his daughter Bilhah his handmaid to be her maid. And he went in also unto Rachel, and he loved also Rachel more than Leah, and served with him yet seven other years. (Genesis 29:10-30)

One of them was named Leah. She had no choice. Her daddy put a veil on her too thick for anybody to see her. She walked down the aisle to be married. When Jacob said, "I do," he was bound. But Rachel was the chosen bride at the beginning. Laban said, "No, I'm going to give you Leah before Rachel because I can't break the cycle of how I do things." He is dealing with flesh and with spirit.

• • •

You say, "I don't understand spirit." Yes, you do because just like Sarah, Rachel was barren. Jacob had to go to Leah to birth anything. Leah gave birth to some sons and Rachel then gave birth to two sons. It was the sons of Leah, representing the flesh, who took Joseph (representing the spirit) and became adverse with him because he had the promise of the father. So Joseph is taken by his brothers, stripped of his coat and thrown in a pit. Makes it look like God's bad, huh. But watch. The sons of Leah were planning on killing Joseph when one of them said, "Let's pull him out of the pit." That one was the last born of Leah. It's very interesting to know that if you follow the name of all of Leah's sons, they were all named based on the flesh except this one. His name was Judah and it means *praise*! And I don't care what pit you find your life in, Judah can get you out!

They pulled Joseph out of that pit. In Genesis 37:26-27 we read, *"And Judah said unto his brethren, What profit is it if we slay our brother, and conceal his blood? Come, and let us sell him to the Ishmeelites, and let not our hand be upon him; for he is our brother and our flesh. And his brethren were content."* They did not know Joseph after the spirit because they came out of a mother of flesh.

"And his brethren were content." Let's keep reading. *"Then there passed by Midianites merchantmen; and they drew and lifted up Joseph out of the pit, and sold Joseph to the Ishmeelites for twenty pieces of silver: and they brought Joseph into Egypt.* (Genesis 37:28) God will allow whatever gives you trouble to show up at the right time, pick you up and move you right where you need to be. "Can I catch ride? Can I get up out of this situation that I'm in? I know you came to push me down, but God's going to use you one day to help me get down the road where I belong!"

• • •

So now, the Bible says that the Father gave birth through Mary's womb. He could not bring Jesus into the world without Him coming through the passage of flesh. As Jesus walked the earth, you have to realize He was a flesh-man. The only thing that God could do was to destroy the flesh in order to get to the spirit. Your redemption was paid for by the flesh. Ishmael had to pay for Joseph's release. Jesus had to pay for your release. *"He was bruised for our iniquities. The chastisement of my our peace was upon Him."* (Isaiah 53:5) And your flesh looked at Jesus and said, "Can I catch a ride?" And Jesus carried your sin, carried your iniquity, carried your problems, carried your troubles all the way to the cross. When He hung His head to die, Jesus said, "It is finished!"

We need to thank God that He let you catch a ride! And just like Judah bringing Joseph up out of that pit where his death was certain, your praise and thanksgiving lifts you out of your own pit into the promise of God for you! Yes, thank you Jesus for letting us catch a ride!

• • •

Chapter 12

Keys to the Gate

In the last chapter we learned some things by taking a look at Jacob. We watched as he was tricked by Laban into marrying Leah before getting to marry Rebeccah, thus ending up like Abraham with two women in his house. But there is much more to be learned through the experiences of this man. Let's pick up another story of Jacob.

And he dreamed, and behold a ladder set up on the earth, and the top of it reached to heaven: and behold the angels of God ascending and descending on it. And, behold, the LORD stood above it, and said, I am the LORD God of Abraham thy father, and the God of Isaac: the land whereon thou liest, to thee will I give it, and to thy seed; And thy seed shall be as the dust of the earth, and thou shalt spread abroad to the west, and to the east, and to the north, and to the south: and in thee and in thy seed shall all the families of the earth be blessed. And, behold, I am with thee, and will keep thee in all places whither thou goest,

• • •

and will bring thee again into this land; for I will not leave thee, until I have done that which I have spoken to thee of. And Jacob awaked out of his sleep, and he said, Surely the LORD is in this place; and I knew it not. And he was afraid, and said, How dreadful is this place! this is none other but the house of God, and this is the gate of heaven. And Jacob rose up early in the morning, and took the stone that he had put for his pillows, and set it up for a pillar, and poured oil upon the top of it. And he called the name of that place Bethel: but the name of that city was called Luz at the first. (Genesis 28:12-19)

The Scriptures tell us that the name Jacob means *supplanter* or *trickster*. He's a liar. On this particular occasion, he's out in the middle of a field. He's running. He's got trouble. He's got trials. He's got adversity. He's got people chasing him. He's been given a wife who's ugly. Then he worked seven more years for another one who was pretty. Everybody's against him. He's hurt. He's aggravated. But know this: Whatever you rest upon will establish you.

Jacob lay down and put his head on a rock. The Word tells us that after he did that, he fell asleep and had a dream. Whatever your mind is laid upon will give you the direction of your future. If your mind stays on negative things, then your imagination will devise a picture of a negative future. Don't rest your head on something that you don't want speaking to you. The Word says that Jacob turned the pillar, the rock, into a pillow. When everything was over and he woke up, the pillow became a pillar. Whatever your mind gets in control and rests upon, that's what your life will be stabilized by. Have you noticed how in the church we have unstable folks who know how to speak in tongues, but they can't talk to their neighbor in love? We know how to sing the songs of Zion, but we can't encourage the woman who works beside us because we're too spiritual for that. We

• • •

know too much about her. We judge before we ever step in and say, "Hey listen, I have to no place to judge you. It's not my position to get into that position." Whatever you rest your mind on, you see, will become what you stabilize your faith with. That's why David said *"Thy word have I hid in mine heart, that I might not sin against thee."* (Psalm 119:11) And that's why Isaiah 26:3 tells us that *"Thou wilt keep him in perfect peace, whose mind is stayed on thee: because he trusteth in thee."*

Jacob lies there asleep and dreams and then finally wakes up from his sleep and makes a declaration. He says, *"Surely, the Lord was in this place and I knew it not"* (verse 16). If you can lay hold to this truth, it will change the way you treat people. You will respond to them differently, act differently, talk and walk differently. It will cause

> **You need to understand that every time God shows up in your situation, He's there to deliver.**

you to think and live in a different way when you realize that, no matter where you go, God is there. The greatest tragedy in your life comes when you awaken and realize that He was there, and you didn't even know it. A millionaire could be standing here with a briefcase full of money ready to hand to you, but if you don't know he's there, you're going to walk away without the money. You need to understand that every time God shows up in your situation, He's there to deliver. He's there to reveal and to protect and to provide. And the worst thing to do is to let God arise, and arise, and you not know He's even there.

Jacob said, "I will call this place—this experience—the house of the Lord. It's not a building, but he called it a house anyway. We know that God doesn't dwell in buildings made by man's hands. No,

• • •

He dwells in the people. He takes residence and He inhabits the praises of His people.

Jacob goes on to say that he saw angels ascending and descending a ladder from heaven to earth. Now, I don't know about you, but I do believe in angels. I don't talk to them every fifteen minutes, and I don't see them riding on the hood ornament of my car on my way home! But I do believe in the dispatching of angels from heaven. Why? Hebrews 1:14, speaking of angels, tells us, *"Are they not all ministering spirits, sent forth to minister for them who shall be heirs of salvation?"* And again in Psalm 91:11 we see, *"For he shall give his angels charge over thee, to keep thee in all thy ways."* For angels to be given charge means they have been given authority to operate on our behalf.

I do believe that. I believe angels have stopped certain things from happening in my life. I believe angels have pushed things out of the way in my life. But here's the tool you need to understand about angels. Their assignment from heaven is to carry messages. Do you remember that Gabriel came to Mary and delivered a message. "Hey Mary! Hey! Wake up! You are highly favored among women! You're going to have a baby!" (See Luke 1:26-31) Yes, there are angels dispatched to bring messages. But bear in mind that they don't just carry something to you. They are always there, too, to make a way back.

In the book of Revelation we know that even now, there are angels before the throne of God singing, "Holy, holy, holy." (Revelation 4:8) Where is God? He's in the midst of that praise. Matthew 18:20 tells us that where two or three are gathered in His name, He is there in the midst of them. That's why two or three people just praising Him will cause God to come right down in the middle of their situation.

• • •

In the beginning of Genesis 28 we read how Jacob's father had blessed him and sent him out with the admonition to not take a wife from Canaan, but to go to Laban in Padan-aram. Jacob was obedient and set out on his journey. Along the way was when he had this dream of the angels. The angels Jacob saw in the dream were ascending and descending. What that meant was that they had something from Jacob to take from here to there so Jacob could have down here what was up there.

There is not a moment when there is not praise going forth in the heavenly realm. There must be praise. So, when we are not praising God, the angels are. Some of you haven't given your angel a coffee break in years! You're letting your angel do all the praising for you. Because of that, there is a lot that God wants to get to you, but it's being held up because your praise is not there. If you will learn that every time you give Him praise your angel can take a breath and bring to you what God has for you. That's when you lift up your voice and begin to give Him the praise and the glory. And your angel collects up what you do and he ascends unto God. And God says, "That's his praise? Here, take this. Now get back down there and give it to him!"

Now, the fact of the matter is that most folks are much more interested in getting a blessing from God than they are in wanting to bless Him. They're not moving forward in their lives. You have to realize that, if you can stand on your feet, you ought to give Him praise. If you can lift your hands, you ought to give Him praise. If you can say, "Thank You," you ought to give Him praise. You shouldn't have to be prodded and told to praise Him. When I think of the goodness of Jesus and all that He's done for me, I can't help but praise Him! I can't hold it back!

• • •

"I have found the gate of heaven," Jacob said. Every gate must have a key. If not, all you're doing is standing and admiring a gate. A gate means access. It's an opening. It means passage, a pathway to get in. In Jacob's day the gates of a city determined its entrance. Anybody who guarded the gate controlled who and what entered into the city.

Every gate has a key. In Revelation 3:7 Jesus says, *"And to the angel of the church in Philadelphia write; These things saith he that is holy, he that is true, he that hath the key of David, he that openeth, and no man shutteth; and shutteth, and no man openeth."* What is the key of David? We see it in Psalm 100:4: *"Enter into his gates with thanksgiving, and into his courts with praise: be thankful unto him, and bless his name."*

> You can turn your situation into a place of praise in an instant, and wherever your praise is, God shows up in your circumstances.

Where exactly is this gate that Jacob was standing before? It isn't just at church because God's omnipresent. Jacob piled stones in the middle of a field and said, "This is it; this is the house of the Lord." The gate for him was right there in the experience. You can turn your situation into a place of praise in an instant, and wherever your praise is, God shows up in your circumstances. And when God shows up, He represents the gate. Jesus said that He was the way, that no one gets to the Father except by Him. (See John 14:6) What determines whether you get through the gate to the other side is the type of gift you are offering unto Him. My Bible says we bring the sacrifice of praise to the house of the Lord (see Jeremiah 33:11).

• • •

There are too many people today waiting to find the praise when they get to the gate. That's not going to get you in. But if you come to the gate with a "thank you," if you come with "I love You, I bless You," you will see that gate swing wide open and you can pass through it! What lies on the other side of that gate doesn't compare with anything on the outside of it!

Thanksgiving and praise are synonymous. They walk together. The words *thanks, thanksgiving,* and *thankfulness* are found in the Bible 258 times. *Praise, praising,* or *praised* are used 107 times. If you do the math, that's 365, which mean that every day of the year, you ought to have a praise, a thanksgiving, or something good on your lips. And that's what gives you access. It's the key for getting you from this dimension to the next dimension.

"Hey, Jesus, we've got a problem! We've got all these people up here, thousands of them, and they're hungry."

Jesus said, "Oh yeah, what do you have with you?"

"What do we have? Nothing big enough! We've got a little bit of money, a little bit of food."

"You mean you think it's insufficient?"

"Yeah, that's what it looks like."

"Hey Peter, what do you have?"

"Oh, I've got a twenty on me, but that's not going to do anything!"

"Well Thomas, what do you have?"

"I don't know what I've got, but I doubt that it'll be enough anyway."

Jesus may have leaned back on that one to scratch his head and think *Why did I even ask that? I knew he was going to doubt it anyway!*

• • •

Finally John pipes up and says, "Hey Jesus, we can't feed everybody, but this little boy over here has a basket with five loaves and two fishes. At least you'll be able to eat a little something."

Jesus says, "Hmm. Bring it to me."

Insufficient. Not enough. Incapable of meeting the present revealed need. Sounds like a lot of situations, doesn't it? Then Jesus took the loaves and fishes in His hands. And He gave thanks. He's holding a little boy's lunch in His hands. What was on this side of the gate wasn't enough. But what lay on the other side of the gate fed the thousands with baskets of leftovers! Nobody there knew the key to getting to the other side of the gate except Jesus. The way He gained access was in standing there and giving thanks.

When you don't see a way out of your situation, when all you see is insignificant and incapable of meeting your present revealed need, know that you have that key of David. Take that key, and give Him the praise, and put that key in the door. Where do I put the praise? "Hey angel, take this and put it at His feet. He is worthy. Everything I need is standing on the other side."

You may be standing in front of something bigger than you right now. I don't know what you're about to step into, but I do know that between you and your miracle has got to be praise. There has to be thanksgiving because what goes up must come down. There is more than enough! Use your key!

• • •

Chapter 13

Building A Habitation of Praise

There is so much to be learned from the stories of the Bible. Some of them are obvious and plain to see. Others are more hidden and their truth must be picked out like precious gems from a mine. But those gems of truths are not buried away from us. They are buried away for us. So it is with the story of the Shunemite woman and her experience with Elisha.

> *And it fell on a day, that Elisha passed to Shunem, where was a great woman; and she constrained him to eat bread. And so it was, that as oft as he passed by, he turned in thither to eat bread. And she said unto her husband, Behold now, I perceive that this is an holy man of God, which passeth by us continually. Let us make a little chamber, I pray thee, on the wall; and let us set for him there a bed, and a table, and a stool, and a candlestick: and it shall be, when he cometh to us, that he shall turn in thither. (2 Kings 4:8-10)*

• • •

Verse nine the Bible says that she *perceived* Elisha was a holy man of God. Are you aware that your level of participation is always geared to your level of perception? You don't involve yourself in things that you don't perceive as being worthy of your input. From this verse we can see that her perception was in the right place. She saw something in him that she wanted to participate in. She said, "Let's build this holy man of God a room and furnish it for him so he can stay here when he comes through town."

We are even told what furnishings went into this room. It had a bed, the place of rest. There was a table, the place of provision. On the table was a candlestick, representing vision and light, being able to see something. A chair was added. The word *chair* in the Bible means *throne* or *seat of judgment*. This woman was saying that they weren't letting him stop by so they could get a blessing. She was letting him stay so that if he had something to correct in their house, he was in a place of authority to tell them whatever he wanted to tell them.

There are some people who are satisfied with God passing by their house, but they don't want Him in their business. They like what they feel when they go to church, but they don't want what's in the church to get into them. It might mess up their personal life or their social life! They want everyone around them to think they're cool. The truth is, you have to build a place in your life where God wants to "turn thither." So this woman said, "Let's build an extension in our house for him."

> *And it fell on a day, that he came thither, and he turned into the chamber, and lay there. And he said to Gehazi his servant, Call this Shunammite. And when he had called her, she stood before him. And he said unto him, Say now unto her, Behold, thou hast been careful for us with all this care; what is to be done for thee? wouldest thou be spoken for to the king, or to the*

• • •

captain of the host? And she answered, I dwell among mine own people. (2 Kings 4:11-13)

The room was finished and the man of God with his servant stopped by. The first thing he did was lie down on the bed. The next thing he did was send for her to ask what he could do for her. Elisha questioned her, "Would you like me to go to the king for you or to the captain of the host?" He was a prophet; he had access to the king. But she told him that she didn't want any of that. She told him she wasn't desiring a level in the kingdom, that she had no desire to move from where she was. Her problem wasn't on the outside. Her problem was on the inside.

You see, you can be driving the right car, living in the right house, but your problem is not about what's on the outside. Your problem is on the inside of you. David said, "Renew my spirit." (See Psalm 51:10) David was saying to God, "Fix that which is on the inside of me. I live in a palace, but my life is in a prison." Can you relate? Maybe you have the money and everything else you need, but there's still something that won't let you sleep at night; it just keeps messing with your mind. God is able to fix what's on the inside of you.

Verse fourteen identifies the problem on the inside of her. *"And he said, What then is to be done for her? And Gehazi answered, Verily she hath no child, and her husband is old."* She was barren and her husband was impotent. Because this woman could not give birth she was considered by the people to be cursed. She had to shop at different times than everyone else. She had to draw water at different times than the others. She could not walk with the women who had children. She was talked about and pointed at when she walked down the street. It's interesting that the Scripture never records her name, but it does record that her perception was right. She had enough understanding that she was able to extend from herself to reach out to Elisha.

• • •

Elisha responded immediately and told Gehazi to call her. Verse 15 says that after she had been called, *"...she stood in the door."* That word *door* means *opening, entrance, gate.* She stood in the gate, in the entrance of the habitation she had built for him. Adding this room onto her house had cost her something to create. She was now standing in the gate of her sacrifice, and it was the place where he dwelt when he passed by.

As the woman stood in the door of his room, Elisha spoke to her and said, *"About this season, according to the time of life, thou shalt embrace a son."* (v. 16) Anything God does, He does in seasons and times. Elisha was saying to her, "Look here, you didn't ask for it, but it's in you to want it. There's a baby coming in the right season at the right time. And this year you're going to have a child."

> ### Anything God does, He does in seasons and times.

Look at her response also in verse sixteen. She said, "Don't play with me. How astonished and yet how excited she must have felt at his words. And in the very next verse we are told that she conceived and bare a son just like Elisha had told her.

> *And the woman conceived, and bare a son at that season that Elisha had said unto her, according to the time of life. And when the child was grown, it fell on a day, that he went out to his father to the reapers. And he said unto his father, My head, my head. And he said to a lad, Carry him to his mother. And when he had taken him, and brought him to his mother, he sat on her knees till noon, and then died.* (2 Kings 4:17-20)

Where did they bring him? This was the promise and it had become a problem; they brought it back to the place where it was

• • •

produced. Nobody knows how to deal with your situation better than you. There are some things in your life that only you can deal with. God wants you to take care of it. He wants you to know that He is able to fix it. So, they bring the boy to his mother, and she held him on her lap until noon, and then he died.

The Bible doesn't record that she said anything. It doesn't record her emotions. Verse 21 simply tells us that she went up, and laid the child on the bed of the man of God, then shut the door and left. She laid him on that bed. It was her house, but she put the child on Elisha's bed.

> *And she called unto her husband, and said, Send me, I pray*
> *thee, one of the young men, and one of the asses, that I may run*
> *to the man of God, and come again. And he said, Wherefore*
> *wilt thou go to him to day? it is neither new moon, nor sabbath.*
> *And she said, It shall be well. (2 Kings 4:22-23)*

Her husband was in the field working. He didn't know that the child was dead and lying in that room. She didn't rehearse the problem with even her husband. Why? She knew that her husband couldn't fix the problem. If you keep bringing issues up before people who can't do anything about them, you're going to continue being disappointed when your situation isn't resolved. Be quiet and realize that if you believe you've laid it on His bed, you can walk away from your problem and say, "It shall be well."

The woman just said, "Get me a donkey and a man who can ride with me to find the man of God." Her husband couldn't figure it out. Why was she running off like that in a hurry in the middle of a workday? She just said back to him, "Listen, it shall be well. Just keep doing what you're doing. It'll be all right."

• • •

Then she left with her driver. She told him to drive and not slow down. Put it in overdrive. She didn't go backward because there was nothing back there to go to. She went straight to the man of God.

So she went and came unto the man of God to mount Carmel. And it came to pass, when the man of God saw her afar off, that he said to Gehazi his servant, Behold, yonder is that Shunammite: Run now, I pray thee, to meet her, and say unto her, Is it well with thee? is it well with thy husband? is it well with the child? And she answered, It is well. (2 Kings 4:25-26)

Elisha saw her coming toward him. He sent Gehazi running out to meet her to find out if everyone was okay. She said, "It is well." When she was leaving the house earlier, her husband had asked her the same thing, and her words to him were, "It *shall* be well." Now her words changed to, "It *is* well." The farther you get from your problem and the closer you get to God, the more your mentality changes.

And when she came to the man of God to the hill, she caught him by the feet: but Gehazi came near to thrust her away. And the man of God said, Let her alone; for her soul is vexed within her: and the LORD hath hid it from me, and hath not told me. (v. 27)

The original translation says that she fell down in a position of worship. She didn't come to God with her finger in His face and saying, "I came here to tell you something." Rather, she came in an attitude of worship and fell at Elisha's feet. When you stop telling God all about your issue and you fall down at His feet in worship, something just happens. You can't move God away from your situation when you're in a position of worship.

Then the woman said to Elisha, *"Did I desire a son of my lord? did I not say, Do not deceive me?"* (v. 28) She said, "Didn't I tell you

• • •

not to play with me?" Some of you are saying, "God why did you give me this, knowing that I'm going to go through this hell? I did not ask You for this! You put it in me. You made me birth it. Now it looks like I've lost it all. You knew all the time this was going to happen when You called me to do this." Instead, like this woman, you need to say, " I don't understand, but I worship You. I praise You. I magnify You."

> *Then he said to Gehazi, Gird up thy loins, and take my staff in thine hand, and go thy way: if thou meet any man, salute him not; and if any salute thee, answer him not again: and lay my staff upon the face of the child. And the mother of the child said, As the LORD liveth, and as thy soul liveth, I will not leave thee. And he arose, and followed her. And Gehazi passed on before them, and laid the staff upon the face of the child; but there was neither voice, nor hearing. Wherefore he went again to meet him, and told him, saying, The child is not awaked.* (2 Kings 4:29-31)

Can you see this scene unfolding? She was down there holding onto him. She heard his instruction to Gehazi and then they all set off toward her house, toward her dead child lying back there on Elisha's bed. This woman told Elisha that she wasn't going to leave him. That comment must have triggered memory in him, back to the day in his own life when a man named Elijah had what Elisha needed. Elijah had told him, "Stay here." (See 2 Kings 2) But Elisha had said to him, "As the Lord liveth, I will not leave you. I'm not going anywhere until I get what I came here for." Elisha had to have remembered how he hadn't asked Elijah for anything. He had come up to Elisha in his field and thrown his mantle on him. Elisha was remembering and thinking, *I didn't find you; you found me.* Memory came up in him of Elijah turning around to him and asking, "What

● ● ●

do you want?" And he recalled his answer, "a double portion." All this memory was firing up in Elisha as they returned to this woman's house.

Gehazi had gone before them and had laid his staff on the boy as he was instructed, but then nothing happened. Sometimes a word from someone else will fix your issue. But there are those times when you're going to have to have Him show up at your house.

Elisha found himself in this woman's house, but the problem was lying on *his* bed! Notice that she laid the problem on what she had already paid for. Your praise is not praise until it costs you something. "We bring the sacrifice of praise into the house of the Lord." (Jeremiah 33:11) When God shows up at your house, He's looking for His bed. "Where is my place of habitation? Where is the place where I dwell? I know this is your house, but when I come here I'm looking for the place that is mine."

He went in therefore, and shut the door upon them twain, and prayed unto the LORD. And he went up, and lay upon the child, and put his mouth upon his mouth, and his eyes upon his eyes, and his hands upon his hands: and he stretched himself upon the child; and the flesh of the child waxed warm. Then he returned, and walked in the house to and fro; and went up, and stretched himself upon him: and the child sneezed seven times, and the child opened his eyes. (2 Kings 4:33-35)

Elisha laid himself down on top of the problem. When you build a place of praise, there ought to come a time when all you see is God. Where's the problem? It's under God. What's God lying on? Your praise! You can't see your problem when you are praising God because He gets between you and the problem! Elisha stretched himself out over the child and the child's body began to warm up.

• • •

Elisha got up, then he went back and stretched himself out on the child again. Now wait a minute! Didn't the child warm up beneath him the first time? Why is this happening like this? What Elisha knew was that he hadn't asked for one shot; he had asked for double. In his mind must have been the thoughts, "I'm not going to give her any less than what I got. So, I'm going to walk back in there."

> *Then he returned, and walked in the house to and fro; and went up, and stretched himself upon him: and the child sneezed seven times, and the child opened his eyes. And he called Gehazi, and said, Call this Shunammite. So he called her. And when she was come in unto him, he said, Take up thy son. Then she went in, and fell at his feet, and bowed herself to the ground, and took up her son, and went out.* (2 Kings 4:35-37)

Do you see that woman built a habitation? It cost her something. It was a sacrifice. She built it; she used it; she took her problem and put it back on the place of praise. It was fixed. She worshipped. That was it. End of story?

Now go forward to chapter eight. Israel had gone into famine. Everyone had lost everything. Nobody had their house, their cattle, or their money. They were dying.

> *And it came to pass at the seven years' end, that the woman returned out of the land of the Philistines: and she went forth to cry unto the king for her house and for her land. And the king talked with Gehazi the servant of the man of God, saying, Tell me, I pray thee, all the great things that Elisha hath done. And it came to pass, as he was telling the king how he had restored a dead body to life, that, behold, the woman, whose son he had restored to life, cried to the king for her house and for her land. And Gehazi said, My lord, O king, this is the woman, and this is her son, whom Elisha restored to life.* (2 Kings 8:3-5)

• • •

Now on this particular day, we see Gehazi telling the king about this woman and her dead son coming back to life. And as he was telling the story, that very woman stood before them to ask the king for her house and land! Is that a coincidence? I don't think so! The king was amazed and appointed an officer to her and declared that she was to be totally restored of all things she had lost since the famine had began. (v. 6)

Now it was her turn to remember back to that room in her house seven years earlier when Elisha had laid himself upon the body of her dead son and life had returned to him. Oh my, that was wonderful. And Elisha had started to walk out of the room, but returned, thinking *I got a double portion. I don't know why I'm doing this, but he needs more than just to be alive.* So he went back and laid on him again and this time the boy sneezed seven times. Oh the double portion! There was a seven year famine coming and the need was met that day in that little room!

Give God your praise today! You might not have a need right now, but the day will come. Your famine will come, and God will bring deliverance and restoration back to your life! The double portion!

• • •

It's All Downhill From Here!

Dead people don't have trouble! That's the only group of folks who can say that! For the rest of us, it seems like our greatest endeavor is to get through life and escape trouble along the way.

Many people go to church thinking that if they get Jesus, they can bypass trouble. They think that if they can be in church, then their troubles are over. But have you ever noticed that about the time you get saved and you've got things moving along right in your life, then out of nowhere something else will pop up unexpectedly? Sometimes it feels like you no sooner get one thing straightened out than something else goes wacky. All of a sudden you find yourself in that stream called life.

God never promised us we wouldn't have trouble. If you're breathing, the Bible guarantees trouble. It says that in this life you will have trials. Trials are meant to prove your innocence. Tribulation—that's trouble. There will be times when people will lie

• • •

about you, speaking all manner of evil against you falsely. When folks start lying about you, you know God's about to do something awesome. It's just right around the corner! And isn't it amazing how we can become so hopeless, even when we have God on our side!

In the Bible, David was a man who God chose to be commander-in-chief of the children of Israel. The reason God picked him was not because David was perfect, but because David was a worshipper. David had a relationship with God and God would rather put responsibility into the hands of a man who knows Him rather than in the hands of a man who thinks he knows everything else. And David got into trouble!

Now, I'm not like David, yet, because if someone tried to kill me with a spear, I don't think I would just say, "Well, sorry you missed. Bless ya! Praise God! See ya next week." Oh no, something in me would go off! I don't think I'd rush to them with a Bible and a CD and say, "I want to bless you." I haven't graduated to that point yet. Sometimes if somebody cuts me off on the interstate, I've got Clint risen up and the Holy Ghost gets in the back seat! That's where you can strap Him in and then He can't affect you anymore. You can just be you. Yes, trouble shows up.

David was in trouble and he began to declare some things. He said, "God will not allow my feet to be moved." (Psalm 121:3) In David's day, the armies didn't have airplanes and ships and sub-marines with torpedoes they could launch from hundreds of miles away. The strength of your army was determined by how many men you had on the ground. Scripture tells us that many times the army of Israel had set itself in array against the enemy. They stood facing in the direction of the battle. One army would stand at one end of a huge field and another nation's army would stand at the other end. And they would advance toward each other and begin to fight.

• • •

As the armies began to fight, the king of each nation would set himself at a particular point in the rear. Then if the enemy began to push the opposing army back, once the advancing army pressed in to a certain point, the king of the weaker army would say, "It's over; we're going to fight another day." Then they would retreat and lose part of their territory to the other nation. When pushed back hard enough, that king would say, "Enough is enough," and they would retreat.

David said, "I'm going to go to battle," and the original Hebrew text says, "...and when I face my enemy, God will not allow my foot to be moved. God comes behind me and when the enemy comes against me, God props me up so the enemy can't push me back." When somebody is behind you, not only can they stop your backward motion, but they can also start pushing you forward against. In other words, what David was saying was, "God's got my back!"

> **If God is behind you, the devil can't push you back into where you used to be!**

If God is behind you, the devil can't push you back into where you used to be! Some of you, the devil would like to push way back to where you used to be, but God says, "I'm going to stand behind you. Your past is gone. Let go of it. Forget those things which are behind you and press toward the mark of the high calling..." (Philippians 3:14) God's got your back!

Behold, he that keepeth Israel shall neither slumber nor sleep. (Psalm 121:4.)

Every nation had watchmen, but David knew that every nation's watchmen were mere men and that sooner or later they needed rest and sleep. And David also knew that when God has my back, He leans over and whispers in my ear, "You can rest on Me because I

don't need any rest." There's just something about having the power to rest on God!

A friend of mine came into town and I wanted to do something nice for him and bless him. So I called ahead to a men's clothing store and arrange with the owner for my friend to come in and shop, but not be charged for anything he wanted. I would take care of the bill myself.

> Sometimes we don't take advantage of what God has already provided for us.

When my friend got to the store, he told the salesman that I had told him to come in. The owner came out and greeted him and said, "Oh yes, we've been expecting you! God bless you!" My friend said that he'd just like to look around, that his budget was a little tight and he didn't know if he'd buy anything or not. But the owner quickly said, "Oh no, no, no. You can just get anything you want. Pastor Brown called ahead of time and said that whatever you picked out, he would take care of it."

The next day I stopped by the store and asked if my buddy had come in. The owner said, "Yes, he did. He was just so nervous and felt so bad." So I asked what he bought. "Oh, he just bought a shirt." Wow, the man was a fool! I mean, if somebody calls ahead of me and I'm told they're going to pay for this, I'm going to say, "I'll take that and that and one of those. Let's see; I'll match it with one of those...." (Ladies, you know what I'm talking about!)

Sometimes we don't take advantage of what God has already provided for us. Sometimes we're fighting things that we should step back and let God take care of because the battle is not ours. The battle is the Lord's!

• • •

David said, "I have something behind me that's stopping the enemy from moving." Then he goes on to say, "He who's watching me doesn't ever slumber or sleep!" Have you ever been going through something and wondered if God was asleep? Your situation is messed up all around you and you're trying to reach God's doorbell to wake him up!

The Lord is thy keeper: the Lord is thy shade upon thy right hand. The sun shall not smite thee by day, nor the moon by night. (Psalm 121:5-6.)

When David was in battle, there was more than just an enemy in front of him fighting against him. There was also an enemy above—the sun—which had a way of pulling the strength out of your body.

If you've ever been an athlete and played football or basketball or baseball, you know there are many times when the coach will say, "If we can stay close until the end of the last quarter we can beat them because we're in better shape than they're in." You see, there's this little thing called dehydration. The sun dehydrates you; it sucks the strength right out of you. Dehydration also affects your equilibrium and your ability to stand.

David is saying, "While my enemy is fighting in the heat of the sun, God is shading me from the elements of the air. No matter where I go, God is covering me so that I'm not dehydrated. I'm not losing my strength!"

The other day I was sitting in my living room watching a documentary. As the interviews were unfolding and they were following these people around, there was a young man with an umbrella in his hands. Everywhere they went, he kept that umbrella over them and while everyone else was sweating and drinking water and

• • •

being miserable, they didn't have to fight the heat because they were under that umbrella.

I heard God say to me, "That's what I'm doing for my people." All those things that get everyone else so upset and agitated and scared and nervous, all those things that zap your ability to stand and be strong, God said that He's a shield over your life to protect you. He's hiding you from the sun!

But how many of you have ever seen elements change in a moment's time? You thought you had just come through trouble and now you're laughing and shouting and dancing, and then you turn around and there's trouble on every hand! That's what the Scripture says. God knows the desert can be 130 degrees in the middle of the afternoon and it can be 30 degrees in the middle of the night. So God says, "Not only do I shield you from the heat, but I will cover you in the cold, in the time you feel like you're all alone, I'm right there."

Do you feel like it's a cold world you're living in and nobody cares? God's going to cover you. God said, "I'm going to keep you; I'm going to hold you; I'm with you. I'm going to make sure nothing happens to you. I'm going to make sure that you don't get hyperthermia. I'm going to make sure that you don't get frozen in the middle of the night and your life fall asleep and your mind be paralyzed and you perish in the middle of a cold situation. I'm going to cover you and keep you warm. I'm going to be your blanket. I'm going to be your umbrella. I'm going to be your shield and your buckler. I'm going to be your head that's lifted up. I'm going to be your guide. I'm going to be your staff. Mercy and grace shall follow you all the days of your life and no weapon formed against you shall prosper. I will be your God!"

• • •

The Lord shall preserve thee from all evil: he shall preserve thy soul. The Lord shall preserve thy going out and thy coming in from this time forth, and even for evermore. (Psalm 121:7-8.)

That word *preserve* is the Hebrew word *shamar* which means *he shall pick me up out of one's reach.* Why wouldn't God just take me out of all this trouble instead of just picking me up above the enemy's reach? The answer is simple. God wants us to see that if it had not been for Him, we might take the credit for it. God is saying, "I'll hold you over it so you can look down on it and give Me praise when it's all over!"

Some of you haven't walked the same path as those around you. You may not have made that wrong decision that someone else made. Because of that, sometimes you want to cast that brother or sister out. You want to kick them out and tell them they're not welcome. We even want to tell them there's no hope for them. We want to ask, "How could you have ever done such a thing?" And we want to judge and say, "You ought to be ashamed of yourself." But God says, "I have a way of picking you up, even when you've been slammed by religious spirits."

People have come to me in alarm and couldn't understand that I let people who sold drugs and had done all kinds of things like that come to church. Yeah, we do! But remember, God had to stand behind you, too. God had to cover you and shield you. God had to pick you up, too! Just because you haven't been put in jail doesn't mean you didn't do anything wrong; it might mean you just didn't get caught! Thank God for grace. Thank God for mercy.

David has told us about God his backup, his protector that needs no rest or sleep, his shield from the sun and covering from the cold, his preservation from the attack of the adversary. Then David says, "He preserves me going out and coming in." You must understand

• • •

that God always puts things in the order of His priorities. He says that it's more important for you to go out than for you to just come in. Where would you be today if someone hadn't come out and given you Truth?

I will lift up mine eyes unto the hills, from whence cometh my help. My help cometh from the Lord, which made heaven and earth. (Psalm 121:1-2.)

David says that when he needs his backup, his shield, his rest, his blanket, his preserver and bodyguard, he looks to the hills. What's up in those hills? Hills alone are just hills, but there's something on the hills.

In Psalm 20: 1-2 we read, "*The Lord hear thee in the day of trouble; the name of the God of Jacob defend thee; Send thee help from the sanctuary, and strengthen thee out of Zion.*" When God instructed David to construct the sanctuary, He said to take all his instruments and all the building materials and build the sanctuary on top of Mount Zion. It is the highest peak in all the land. God told David that there would come days when he would find himself in valley experiences. God wanted him, when feeling hopeless and ready to give up, to be able to turn and look to the highest point and focus on that sanctuary because out of that sanctuary God would send strength.

God was saying to David, "It's going to take everything you've got to climb this mountain, to get to this sanctuary, but the effort of climbing doesn't compare to the momentum when you come down! So David, after you have a sanctuary experience, it's all down hill from there. Everything you're going to face, you'll face with momentum and when you do, "I'm going to have your back and I'm going to shelter you from the sun. And I'm going to keep you from the cold and I'm going to preserve you from the attack. I'm going to guard you on your way out and on your way in.

• • •

O God, thou art my God; early will I seek thee: my soul thirsteth for thee, my flesh longeth for thee in a dry and thirsty land, where no water is; To see thy power and thy glory, so as I have seen thee in the sanctuary. Because thy lovingkindness is better than life, my lips shall praise thee. (Psalm 63:1-3)

I will meditate also on all thy work, and talk of thy doings. Thy way, O God, is in the sanctuary: who is so great a God as our God? Thou art the God that doest wonders: thou hast declared thy strength among the people. (Psalm 77:12-14.)

For all the gods of the nations are idols: but the Lord made the heavens. Honour and majesty are before him: strength and beauty are in his sanctuary. (Psalm 96:5-6.)

Behold, bless ye the Lord, all ye servants of the Lord, which by night stand in the house of the Lord. Lift up your hands in the sanctuary, and bless the Lord. (Psalm 134:1-2.)

In a time when you don't know what's going to happen, stand. In a time when you're unsure, stand. Where? In the sanctuary. Everything you need is in the sanctuary.

The Bible says they beat Jesus in the city streets of Jerusalem and they put a cross on his back. But they made a mistake! They let Him be crucified, not in a valley, not in a graveyard. They let Him climb a hill called Golgotha. Jesus states, *"If I be lifted up from the earth, I will draw all men unto me."* (John 12:32) They put Him on a hill and Jesus said, "Beat me now. Stab me now. Crucify me now, but it's all down hill from here. What's down hill? They pierced His side and blood came down hill.

• • •

But there's something wrong with this text. David said, "I will look unto the H-I-L-L-S plural, but the temple was constructed on only one hill. David is looking through a microscope of prophetic vision and he sees hills when all he saw in the natural was a hill. After Jesus died, the prophetic voice came true. Jesus had already said that you are a city set on a hill that cannot be hid (Matthew 5:14). Paul said, too, that the sanctuary is not made by hands, but you are the temple of the Holy Ghost (2 Corinthians 5:1, 1 Corinthians 6:19).

I believe that what David saw was thousands of years ahead of time. He saw you. He saw me. He saw hills everywhere. We are the hills. When somebody needs to have a backup, they should be able to find it in the church! When somebody needs someone to pick them up, they ought to find that in the church.

• • •

Chapter 15

Just Give Him the Praise

We are so blessed to have the wisdom and insight of David and his life experiences. When you read the stories of his life, his transparency is obvious and he affords us an awesome look into the heart and thoughts of the one called *a man after God's own heart.* Part of what endears David to us is his human qualities, his courage, his mistakes, his strengths, and his weaknesses. It's not difficult to learn from David because he is not so very different from each of us in many ways. His whole life is a testament to praising and worshipping God, even in the midst of his errors and difficult life situations. He repented and praised and kept on going.

In Psalm 132:1-5 we hear the words of David:

LORD, remember David, and all his afflictions: How he sware unto the LORD, and vowed unto the mighty God of Jacob; Surely I will not come into the tabernacle of my house, nor go up into my bed; I will not give sleep to mine eyes, or slumber to

• • •

mine eyelids, Until I find out a place for the LORD, an habitation for the mighty God of Jacob.

We understand that the sanctuary is no longer a building made by man's hands. The sanctuary is now New Testament sanctuary; we are the temple of the Holy Spirit. The Bible tells us that God dwells in Judah. Psalm 114:2 says, *"And Judah was His sanctuary."*

So we understand that if Judah is His sanctuary and Judah means *praise*, and if I am the temple of the Holy Spirit, then if praise dwells in me, I am God's sanctuary. Psalm 114 goes on to tell us that the Red Sea saw it and rolled back. The Jordan saw it and ran out of its way. The hills saw it and it skipped out of its way. That tells me that my adversary or problem situation should never be a match to my praise. My issue should never be a match to my praise. Why? From the first moment they meet, my praise should intimidate my issue enough to get it out of my way!

Don't allow your circumstances to overtake your imagination to the point where you feel inadequate and no match for your problem. As you really begin to know who you are and to embrace who you are, then you understand that the battle is really not even yours to fight (2 Chronicles 20:15). You'll know that all you have to do is just give God the praise. In every situation, the Bible doesn't even give a rest time when we can stop praising. David again in Psalm 34:1 tells us to bless the Lord at all times and to let His praises continually be in our mouths. That's what David did!

Every day you live you are going to face challenging situations, but you don't have to let them steal your praise. When you make that choice, your praise will catapult you through every problem that arises in your life. You will move on into destiny and purpose. The best is still yet to come in your life!

• • •

I am both saddened and challenged when I realize that we as Christians should be the most powerful, dynamic, and positive people on the face of the earth. But we are not. There are so many of us who seem almost powerless, lacking in hope or vision. What we seem to have an abundance of in our midst is complaining and murmuring and crying about everything we don't have or don't like. And we stay where we are because we don't realize that our complaint has as much power as our praise. God didn't say He would inhabit our complaints. God dwells in your praise.

> **God is perpetual, never ending, never stopping. He's always looking for a sanctuary of praise in you.**

The only thing God really desires for a dwelling place is your praise. Psalm 132:13-14 says this so plainly:

> *For the LORD hath chosen Zion; he hath desired it for his habitation. This is my rest for ever: here will I dwell; for I have desired it.*

In your Bible, whether Old Testament or New Testament, Hebrew or Greek, the meaning of the word *here* is simply *here*. Now, that may not sound like such a deep revelation at first glance, but it really is! Wherever you are is *here*. Wherever I am I'm *here*. You are not *there*. Too many people want to go *there* and forget that they are *here*. They say things like, "If I could just get *there*, I'd be different," or "When I get *there* my problems will be over." The trouble with that line of thinking is that, when you get *there*, you're still just *here*.

God is perpetual, never ending, never stopping. He's always looking for a sanctuary of praise in you. When your tough situation comes, you are to be offering up your praise to Him. When you

• • •

make the next move, you are to be offering up your sacrifice of praise to Him, trusting that He is working out all the unseen things for your good. But when that tough situation comes and you don't praise Him in the midst of it, your mind will become clouded over with fear and hopelessness. At the point when you refuse to praise Him is the point when you cease to experience Him in your midst.

Yes, when you lay down your praise based on your problem, God keeps moving, but you're still sitting in your situation wondering where God is. Where is God? He's still in your praise! He never left there. What you have to do is go back and pick up your praise from wherever you left it. Start giving Him your praise; that's where He is. And that's when deliverance starts showing up. That's when abundance starts showing up. That's when blessing starts showing up.

Look again at Psalm 132. We've seen that Zion is His habitation. God said it was his rest forever because it was His desire. Now look at what verse fifteen tells us: *I will abundantly bless her provision...* He is referring to the place where He dwells as a "her." That doesn't mean that praise is feminine or that your praise is a female. It does mean that He called the sanctuary where His praise resides a "her" because it's a prophetic outlook of who we are. We are the bride of Christ (Revelation 21:2).

So in this psalm we are seeing that God dwells in us because we are the sanctuary. And God says to us, "While I'm there, I will abundantly bless her provision." The word *abundantly* means *more than you have the ability to deal with*. The word *bless* means *provision for the process*. That's exciting! That's God saying to you, "Whatever process you're going through right now, I'm providing everything it takes to survive and to be successful in that process." God will take care of you through the process. Aren't you glad God doesn't bail out when trouble shows up? All you have to do is just give Him some praise.

• • •

"I'm going through hell."

"Praise Him!"

"I'm facing bankruptcy."

"Praise Him!"

"I don't know where I'm going to turn."

"Praise Him!"

"I don't know how I'm going to get out of this."

"Praise Him!"

It's better than crying about it. It's better than complaining about it. Don't call everybody you know and tell them what you're going through. Why don't you call everybody you know instead and say, "Hey, you know where I am, but I'm getting ready to get up and get out of this situation!"? Just praise Him!

I will clothe her priests with salvation. (Psalm 132:16)

The word *clothe* here means *to arm, to surround or array, to come upon, to put on, or to put upon.* All of those meanings are good, but the best translation is this, *to cover in transition.* In other words, God knows that you are at point A and headed for point B, and you are clothed in salvation. That does not mean to blanket with restriction, but rather, it means *to observe and walk with.* So, as you're in transition from point A to B, He always keeps you in His reach. He covers you.

We are instructed to put on the whole armor of God in Ephesians 6:11. The purpose for it is so we can stand against the fiery darts of the enemy. Look at the pieces of the armor and notice that they cover every part of the body except one. There's the breast-plate of righteousness, the helmet of salvation, the shield of faith, the sword of the Spirit. Your feet are shod with the preparation of

• • •

the gospel of peace. But notice none of the armor covers your back. The reason for that is because God's got your back! You don't have to worry about the issues and situations of life; He's there!

He will cover during transition. Let us shout for joy! In that day, the army of victory did not shout for joy until the battle was over. It was an even greater humiliation than losing if you first shouted as

> You don't have to worry about the issues and situations of life; He's there!

the victor and later lost. God is telling us that, when it comes to the devil standing in your face, you don't owe him one second of respect. All you have to do when he comes in is start shouting and praising God. Let the devil know that you're not waiting until the battle's over because it's not even your battle anyway. Tell him, "I'm going to shout now because God's already fought and won the battle for me. I'll just give Him some praise right here in the middle of it!"

"There will I make the horn of David to bud: I have ordained a lamp for mine anointed." (Psalm 132:17) David's horn is his head. David was the one who was rejected and pushed aside by his brothers. David was the one not put in the lineup to be the next king of Israel when Samuel came to choose somebody. But David's father was standing there knowing that this was not all of his sons. David was the only one of them whose mother was in the lineage of Jacob. You may be at the back of the line with everyone in front of you, but God can take you from that place and bring you all the way to the front of the line because of your praise. If you want to come out of where you are and enter into a chosen situation with vision and purpose and destiny, give God a praise here and now.

"His enemies will I clothe with shame: but upon himself shall his crown flourish." (Psalm 132:18) Do you see that the battle is really not yours? The battle is truly the Lord's. God showed David that He lives in the atmosphere of praise. God will not live in an environment that does not practice praise.

You can name it and claim it, blab it and grab it all you want, but it is not going to come if you don't know how to praise Him. David said that when he got there, she was abundantly blessed. She couldn't even deal with the increase. She was being covered in transition. She was being anointed and chosen above everybody else. She was shouting for joy before the battle even started. Now look again at verse eighteen. It would still have been great if it had said, "…and her enemy will I…." But that's not what it says. It says, "HIS enemies…" Oh, you thought the devil was coming after you, but God said, "This is my battle; this is a personal issue of Mine. I'll handle this."

I want you to get this! Look at this picture. I've got God with me. He's blessing me abundantly. He covers me everywhere I go. With every move I make He covers me. He's here for me. When I get into situations where I don't think I can make it out, He reaches down and pulls me out of my circumstance. It's because of my praise! As long as I give Him the praise, then He's blessing me, covering me, anointing me, and raising me up. When the devil shows up, God has my back. Because of my praise, at that moment God taps me on the shoulder and says, "Just get behind Me because this battle's not yours. And you can start shouting now because it's a done deal!" Just give Him some praise and watch your world begin to change!

• • •

• • •

Chapter 16

How's Your Night Life?

Perception is a powerful thing. Sometimes I think it's difficult to understand what God thinks about a particular topic. All my life I was told by a preacher how God thought about me, but I never could find it in my Bible. It was just their perception of how God is.

I grew up thinking of God as sitting on the throne with a baseball bat and a shotgun. That way, if He couldn't reach you, He could shoot you! That's what happened if you did anything wrong. Wrong wasn't about stabbing folks or stealing stuff. Wrong was doing things like going to the movies. Wrong was just having a TV in your house. You could have a monitor and rent movies, but you couldn't have a real TV with channels coming in on it. We couldn't watch TV. That was the one-eyed devil. So, we never missed going along to conferences so we could stay in hotels and watch the tube. And every Sunday afternoon we witnessed to our neighbors…so we could watch football on TV. We were always careful to witness during halftime!

• • •

Women couldn't wear pants. I'm not talking about to church; I'm talking about anywhere. So my sisters and friends would roll up their pants legs and wear long skirts so my daddy would see them getting on the bus with a skirt. But when they got on the bus, they'd take those skirts off, roll down their pants legs and look like everybody else—sinners going to hell.

Women couldn't wear makeup. Hmm. Couldn't put on any eye shadow or lipstick. Why? They'd go to hell. I grew up and found out the truth: You just *look* like hell without makeup on!

All of this created a pretty warped perception in me of what God was really like, what holiness was really like. So, I learned way back to check out God's perceptions and His slant on things for myself. This is especially true in instances where God gives something a name. I want to know what He was thinking when He did that.

Behold, bless ye the LORD, all ye servants of the LORD, which by night stand in the house of the LORD. Lift up your hands in the sanctuary, and bless the LORD. The LORD that made heaven and earth bless thee out of Zion. (Psalm 134)

When you read the Scriptures, you must understand that you read them from the progression in which activities of that time were happening. Don't just read a verse, but also read the verse above it, or the chapter above or beneath it. Find the context, where that passage came from and where it's going.

He tells us to *"bless the Lord, all ye servants of the Lord, which by night stand in the house of the Lord."* (v. 1) Now, I have a question for you. "How's your night life?"

In the beginning God created the heaven and the earth. And the earth was without form, and void; and darkness was upon the face of the deep. And the Spirit of God moved upon the face of

• • •

the waters. And God said, Let there be light: and there was light. And God saw the light, that it was good: and God divided the light from the darkness. And God called the light Day, and the darkness he called Night. And the evening and the morning were the first day. (Genesis 1:1-5)

When we look at the word *night*, I am compelled to find out God's perception and perspective on this name. Notice in this part of the creation account of Genesis that God saw that the light was good and He separated the light from the darkness. He said that the darkness would have its place and the light would have its place. Then He said that the light would be called *day*. And He called the darkness *night*. Pretty basic, huh. Evening came and then the morning came.

When we talk about *night*, we must revert back to God's original perception of what night was. If God saw something and called it a certain name, then even if it wasn't that before He named it, it was after He named it! God cannot lie. It didn't say that He couldn't tell a lie. It said He cannot lie because the minute God says it, it becomes true. That's why if you call me a loser and I am a loser, the moment God says, "You're a winner," it doesn't matter what I was before; I'm a winner when God calls me one. If you call me a sinner and God calls me redeemed, I don't care what you saw me as; I am redeemed.

So, when we see night here, I understand that night is accompanied by various characteristics that make it what it is. He said it was formless, which tells me it had no potential in and of itself to do anything. It is darkness. It is also empty. It is uncertainty. Now when I say empty, void, formless, uncertainty, when I say darkness, my question to you is: Have you ever been there before? Have you ever been in that place where nothing made sense to you? You didn't know why you were going through this issue. Nothing was certain

• • •

to you. You didn't know how it was going to turn out. It was dark. You couldn't see your way out. You were hopeless, empty, and void.

The truth is, we've all been there. How do I know? I know because day doesn't last twenty-four hours! Thirteen hours is all you get, then you're going to experience a night. I'm talking reality here. There are too many folks out there who think that because they have Jesus, they aren't going through anything. These are those who have a fever, red eyes, a headache, and can't get out of bed. But when you ask them, "Are you sick?" they shoot back, "No!" You liar! We don't get to skip through life and skip all the "stuff." Romans 4:17 didn't say to call those things that are as though they are not. It said to call those things that be not as though they are. Big difference.

> God has a way of doing things in our nighttime experiences.

It's okay to be sick and say, "I'm sick." And also add to that, "But this is not going to last forever." It's okay to have cancer and say, "I've got cancer." But also add to it, "By His stripes I am healed." It's okay to be broke and say, "I'm broke." But say, "Hey, He gives me the power to get wealth." It's okay to be down and say, "I'm down." But also tell people, "I will arise, and I will come out of this mess." Do you have a night life?

God has a way of doing things in our nighttime experiences. Joseph, in the darkness of the pit and the darkness of the prison, was prepared for the lifestyle of the palace. Abraham was put to sleep so that he could see that his present wasn't all there was to his future. Jacob went to sleep and woke up with a different name and identity. He was no longer known as the *deceiver*, but as Israel, the *the prince* and representation of God. Elijah went into the darkness of the cave to hear, not an earthquake or a fiery shot from heaven, but

• • •

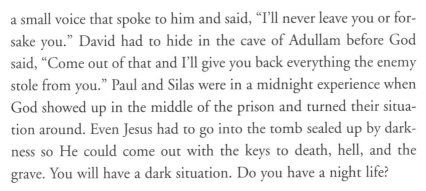

a small voice that spoke to him and said, "I'll never leave you or forsake you." David had to hide in the cave of Adullam before God said, "Come out of that and I'll give you back everything the enemy stole from you." Paul and Silas were in a midnight experience when God showed up in the middle of the prison and turned their situation around. Even Jesus had to go into the tomb sealed up by darkness so He could come out with the keys to death, hell, and the grave. You will have a dark situation. Do you have a night life?

Yes, you're going to walk through some darkness. It doesn't matter how much money you have. You can be worth millions or billions of dollars and still not be able to get to sleep at night, having to take prescription drugs to get to sleep at night and pouring Scotch in a glass when morning comes to wake up and get going. Throw a little cocaine in for good measure somewhere in the day. No, money can buy you things, but it can't buy you peace of mind. It can buy sex, but it can't buy love. It can buy a house, but it can't buy a home. You can walk through some nighttime situations and have the nice car and live in the biggest house in town. People are wondering why you're unhappy. It's because you can be in a nighttime experience and the light is shining all around you.

What do you do when you're in a nighttime experience? How do you survive whenever you're in uncertainty, and emptiness, and everything is void, and you can't see your way out? What are your options when you don't think you have any? Have you ever had it all together on the surface and everything is falling apart beneath you? What do you do?

He says, "Behold...." Wait a minute. Night is a time of darkness, yet God is telling me to *behold*. That word *behold* means *to focus on what is being unveiled*. It's called revelation. I can gain revelation, even in my dark times of life. I found out that if I was never

• • •

sick, I would never know Him as healer. If I had never been abandoned, I would never know Him as a friend who sticks closer than a brother. If I had never been broken, I would never know Him as a mender of broken people. If I had never been weak, I would never know Him as strength through joy. If I had never been attacked, I would never know Him as a shield and a buckler. If I had never been talked about, I would never know Him as a defender of the brethren. If I had never been accused, I would never know Him as a judge of mercy and grace. If I had never been in warfare, I would never know Him as no weapon formed against you shall prosper.

You can see things in your nighttime experience. But you can only see after it's over, when the light comes on. So He separated the darkness from the light. The good thing is, evening came, and then daytime showed up. Evening comes and evening goes. David caught this when he said, *"Weeping may endure for a night, but joy comes in the morning."* (Psalm 30:5)

God was talking to my heart one day and He said, "Midnight doesn't last an hour. Midnight lasts only sixty seconds. I can turn your situation around in sixty seconds." I thought about the truth in that. In seconds we go from nighttime to daytime. Weeping endures only in the night. God brings you to a nighttime experience because if you could see everything that was coming against you, He knows you would turn around and run.

So God lets you walk along in the dark, temporarily blinded so you cannot see your adversary. And He says the only thing you can rely on is the fact that your faith comes by hearing, and hearing by the word of God. (See Romans 10:17) Everything God created He created out of darkness. So He fights for you. (Exodus 14:13) When the battle is over, God comes and lifts the scales off of your eyes. Then you see the adversary.

• • •

You have to stand in the midnight hour and bless the Lord. Don't run from the house; run to it. When trouble shows up, bless the Lord. When darkness shows up, bless the Lord. Bless the Lord at all times! Yes, we can stand in the house of God. I can stand in God's house. It doesn't make much sense! I ought to kill myself, but I'm still standing! I ought to quit, but I'm still standing! I ought to throw in the towel, but I'm still standing! I'm just going to stand here and praise Him all night long! How's your night life?

• • •

• • •

Chapter 17

A Simple Thank You Will Do

Have you noticed that we seem to be in a generation of thankless people? There are so many people constantly focused on what they have or want. There is no time spent in gratitude for what we do possess in our lives. We are people who remember our pain more than we do our victories. We remember our struggles more than we remember our successes. It's so easy for us to live in a state of depression because we live in a nation that is overrun with the information of pain, and wars, and struggle, and abuse, and trouble. Everyone's going through it. What's amazing is that the poorest people in America would be some of the richest people in other places in the world. I would like to take you to the Sudan. I would like to take you to some of these third world countries where, if they have a dirt floor and a roof over the house, they consider themselves in a middle-class community. How can we here in America feel so deprived and so depressed? It produces a constant state of complaining.

"You have a job."

• • •

"Yeah, but it doesn't pay enough."

"You've got a car to drive."

"Yeah, but it's not new."

"You have a house to live in."

"Yeah, but it's really kind of old and the carpet is stained."

"Well, you've got a wife."

"Yeah, but…."

"You've got a husband."

"Yeah, but I wish I didn't."

"You've got kids!"

"Well, they're just full of the devil."

"You have friends."

"They all talk about me."

There just aren't many of us out there who are grateful for what we have. We tend to mark our happiness and fulfillment and thankfulness based on comparing ourselves with those around us. We frequently find ourselves greatly lacking and then we strive for more…of anything and everything. The easiest way to depress ourselves is to consistently look at somebody else who we think is better off than we are. Their stuff looks better than ours. The grass is always greener on the other side, it seems.

But I'm telling you, you can have a million dollars in the bank, but be bankrupt of peace. You can have a ten thousand square-foot house, but live in an empty home. You can't put a price on those things that truly fulfill your life. We can put a price on a diamond, or a car, or a house, or a dress, or shoes. Think about this, though.

• • •

What price would you be willing to put on your ability to walk somewhere? How much money would you pay for the ability to see your children grow up? How much would you be willing to pay to hear your child say, "I love you"? How much would you be willing to pay for the ability to be able to feel when you touch, to taste when you eat? You don't even realize how wealthy you really are. Instead, you say, "If I had a million dollars I'd be happy." Would you take a million dollars for your sight?

> **Thankfulness is not a natural instinct. It comes from our cultivating it.**

Depression seems to be all around us. I was in Los Angeles, driving through million-dollar neighborhoods. The houses had bars on the windows because of people burglarizing and stealing their property. People live in fear, and they're ungrateful for things.

Thankfulness is not a natural instinct. It comes from our cultivating it. Thankfulness is something that a parent puts into you. Do you remember when you were a kid and someone would give you something, what happened? Somebody—your momma or daddy—would say, "What do you say?" It was something you were brought up with. It is something that is passed down.

I wonder about some of the next generation because they're so used to getting everything they want, when they want it, how they want it, and we've not taught them to be grateful for what they have. We go into communities and we build expensive gymnasiums with nice goals and nice floors and nice fencing around things. But when you go back into those same communities a year later the goals are bent, and the nets are gone, and the fence is torn down, and there's debris everywhere, and people are painting on the court. Why is that? I wonder if it's not because we are rarely thankful for what we've never had to pay for.

• • •

See, if it cost you something to be here, then you understand how powerful it is to understand how blessed you really are. I can tell you, you are blessed more than you think you are. I don't care if you don't have a job. There's a job waiting on you just across the street. I don't care if you don't have a car. You can still see and walk and somebody will drive you where you need to go. You are blessed.

Now thanks be unto God who always causes us to triumph. Whatever you are fighting, you are going to win! It doesn't matter what's coming against you, you're going to make it. No weapon formed against you will prosper. Give thanks with a grateful heart. Bless the Lord at all times. Keep His praise continually in your mouth! Give thanks to the Lord and don't forget His benefits. He's been good to me. He's been good to you. When I think of the goodness of Jesus, I just have to say thank you!

We are so used to mechanical praise. But my Bible says to *make* a joyful noise. You don't know how to praise Him until you're by yourself at the house and something just moves on the inside of you. You start looking around at where you could be, and at where you are. You walk around your house. Maybe you grab a picture of your kids and walk around the house carrying the picture with you and saying, "Thank you, Lord. They could be in jail. They could be in the hospital. They could be in the ground. But thank You. They're not perfect, but You bless their coming in and You bless their going out. Minister to them, Lord. Anoint them. Keep Your hand on them. Put a wall around them. Protect them. Guide them. Thank you for my kids!" When it all comes right down to it, you don't need the shirt on your back. You don't need the shoes on your feet. But I thank God for what He's done in my soul, in my spirit. I wouldn't take a million dollars for the peace He brings me in the middle of the night. Thank you, Lord!

• • •

God doesn't need our money. He doesn't need our cars. He couldn't sit in your car. He sits on the circumference of the universe and the earth is His footstool. We don't have anything God needs. But we do have something He desires. He just wants us to give Him thanks. He wants us to lift our hands and thank Him! A simple thank you will do!

Think about how good He is to you. How many times has He wrapped His arms around you and held you through the night? We are to enter His gates with thanksgiving in our hearts and enter His courts with praise. (Psalm 100:4-5) Why? Because God is good. That word *good* means *bondsman*. When you got yourself in it, He came. He didn't just get you out of it; He paid something to get you out. When you broke the law and you deserved to be where you are, Somebody came and bailed you out. Have you ever been bailed out of a situation? I'm not talking about jail. I'm talking about being bailed out in your life.

I am reminded again of the woman who came to Jesus and knelt at his feet and broke her alabaster box of precious ointment, and washed his feet with her tears and wiped them with her hair. (See Luke 7:37) Somebody asked her why she was there. Her response would have been, "Because I'm not supposed to be here." That does not make so much sense until you see the bigger picture. She remembered that it wasn't long ago that some men had grabbed her. They caught her in adultery, and took her, and threw her at Jesus' feet. And she had to be thinking now, "I received my pardon at His feet; I'll release my praise there, too." What an amazing act of gratitude and thankfulness.

The only difference between her and the crowd of men was simply that she got caught. It's the only difference because Jesus told the men that if any of them felt like they'd never been involved in something

• • •

they shouldn't have, that He wanted to know it so He could watch them throw the first rock at her. They waited and when no rock was thrown, it proved that her getting caught was the only difference between her and them.

Judas wanted the oil to have been sold and turned into money. But Jesus told him, "I don't want her money; I don't want your money. A simple thanks will do. If you could just stop and take the time like this woman did to remember where I brought you from. All I want is a simple thanks."

> Learning how to be grateful is the greatest act of gratitude a person could have.

Just a simple thank you. Learning how to be grateful is the greatest act of gratitude a person could have. I opened a door for a lady and she said, "Oh, you opened the door because I'm a woman and you think you need to open it?" I answered, "No, I opened the door because I'm a gentleman. (She could have used a little gratitude and thankfulness herself!)

Stop listing what you want and what you don't have. Take five minutes to write down what you wouldn't take any amount of money for and see how truly rich you are! In the society in which we live, we say that everything has a price. But that's because we're conditioned to think that way.

What about the things you cannot change and that God will never fix? There are blind people in the world who will never ever see. They will die blind. Others will die deaf, lame. Everybody in your family had beautiful babies, and you had a baby born with Down Syndrome. Can God heal him? Yes. Will he get healed? We don't know. You might have to live with that the rest of your life. He might have a mental and physical struggle.

• • •

I look at the things that I cannot change and that God will never fix and I ask Him, "Give me strength to endure. Give me the courage to stand through the test of time." And I give Him thanks now, even in the middle of what I don't understand. Oh God, when I was about to fall, You let me lean on You. Thank You. When I fell, You reached down and picked me up. Thank You. All He requires is a thank you. Take the time to remember how good God has been to you. A simple thank you will do!

• • •

...

About the Author

An anointed preacher and motivational speaker, Pastor Brown is an accomplished musician and songwriter. He has written and published over 250 praise and worship songs, some of which have been recorded and performed in five different languages. Pastor Clint's music is known worldwide with 14 albums, some of which have remained in the top 10 of Praise and Worship Distribution Charts. Pastor Brown's latest project, "Mercy & Grace" released in July 2005.

Pastor Brown is the CEO of Tribe Music Group Inc., which owns and operates a first class recording studio and a highly profiled publishing company and distribution company.

In less than 10 years Pastor Brown has seen his congregation grow to over 6,000 members and cover many pastors and churches throughout America. FaithWorld is a multi-racial church with over 30 different nationalities represented in its membership.

Pastor Brown oversees 2 major conferences each year: JUDAH, a music conference which reaches thousands worldwide; and I.P.L.C., a pastor's and leadership conference which hosts over 500 churches teaching keys to leadership and ministry.

• • •

His message is clear: "Praise brings change to every situation in your life, and worship is the relationship with the Life Giver." Pastor Brown has been met with triumph and tragedy in his life, and has found that praise provides victory, and worship sustains you through any trials you may face.

• • •